OUR FRAGILE PLANET

THE WASTE CRISIS

Jenny Tesar

Series Editor:
Bernard S. Cayne

A Blackbirch Graphics Book

Facts On File

Facts On File, Inc.
460 Park Avenue South
New York, NY 10016
USA

Library of Congress Cataloging-in-Publication Data
Tesar, Jenny E.
    The waste crisis.
    (Our fragile planet; 2/by Jenny Elizabeth Tesar; series editor, Bernard S.
Cayne.)
    Includes bibliographical references and index.
    Summary: Examines all kinds of waste, including commercial, industrial,
toxic, and radioactive waste, and discusses the problems and possible solutions
connected with existence and management of such pollutants.
    ISBN 0-8160-2491-X
    1. Refuse and refuse disposal—Juvenile literature. 2. Sewage—Juvenile
literature. 3. Hazardous wastes—Juvenile literature. [1. Refuse and refuse
disposal. 2. Sewage. 3. Hazardous wastes. 4. Pollution.] I. Title. II. Series:
Tesar, Jenny E. Our fragile planet; 2.
TD792.T47 1991
363.72'8—dc20   90-47294

A British CIP catalogue record for this book is available from the British
Library

Facts On File books are available at special discounts when purchased in bulk
quantities for businesses, associations, institutions or sales promotions. Please
call our Special Sales Department in New York at 212/683-2244 (dial 800/322-
8755 except in NY, AK, or HI) or in Oxford at 865/728399.

Design: Blackbirch Graphics, Inc.

Printed and Manufactured in the United States of America.

10 9 8 7 6 5 4 3 2

This book is printed on acid-free paper.

CONTENTS

1
THE WASTE CRISIS

IT weighs more than 230 billion basketballs. If we could convert IT into basketballs, there would be 43 basketballs for every single person on Earth.

IT weighs more than 32 million African elephants. If we could convert IT into elephants, Africa's endangered elephant population would be 53 times greater than it actually is.

IT weighs more than six times as much as all the plastics produced in the United States this year. But if we converted IT into plastics, IT would probably be bigger than ever!

IT is America's garbage.

Each year, Americans discard 160 million tons, or 320 billion pounds (145 billion kilograms), of garbage. That is more garbage than any other country in the world. It is even more than China, which has four times as many people.

Eggshells, potato peelings, empty cartons, soap suds, paper towels, shoes, plastic pens, broken chairs and toilet wastes come from people's homes. Grass clippings, leaves and weeds come from their gardens. Used oil, carburetors and tires come from their cars and trucks.

Industries and government facilities add millions of tons of other wastes. Hospitals throw out blood, diseased body parts, syringes and bandages. Builders have construction debris. Factories discard thousands of poisonous chemicals. Nuclear power plants produce radioactive wastes.

Opposite page:
Vehicular wastes—which include millions of scrapped cars, buses, trucks and other commercial vehicles—compose a large part of the wastes produced by industrial nations.

None of these wastes are unique to the United States. Everywhere, the Earth is being dirtied with people's wastes. In Thailand, the River of Kings carries rotting garbage and human excrement. In Bulgaria, a giant steel plant at Kremikovci dumps 20,000 tons of dust and grime a year on the nation's capital of Sofia. In Mexico, shantytowns have no running water and no sanitation; garbage and human wastes form stinking piles where rats roam freely. In Canada, radioactive substances leak from uranium mine wastes and contaminate rivers.

Accidents create wastes, too. A serious automobile accident may damage a car so badly that it is beyond repair. When a Soviet nuclear submarine carrying two nuclear weapons sank off Norway in 1989, the number of nuclear warheads on the ocean floor rose from 48 to 50. After a 1986 fire at a chemical warehouse in Basel, Switzerland, some 30 tons of pesticides were released into the Rhine River.

Despite clean-up efforts, stricter laws and more efficient technology, the situation is becoming worse. More and more wastes are being produced. Yet there are few ways to get rid of them. No disposal method is attractive. They all pollute the environment. Dumping wastes into waterways contaminates drinking water and poisons fish. Dumping wastes in landfills threatens to contaminate underlying groundwater. Burning wastes reduces their volume but presents the danger of emitting poisonous chemicals into the atmosphere. And the ashes that remain are poisonous, creating another disposal problem.

One of the basic causes of the waste crisis is the world's rapidly growing population. More than 5.3 billion people live on Earth. Every second of every day, three people are born. Every year, there are 90 million more people. By the end of this century, over 6 billion people will live on Earth, all producing wastes.

Another cause is growing industrialization: more and more factories producing more and more goods for more and more people. In developed nations, particularly the United States, the desire to consume and the demand for convenience spur

A GROWING MOUNTAIN

Each and every day, the residents of New York City discard more than 13,000 tons of garbage. Over the course of a year, that adds up to more than 4.8 million tons, or 9.6 billion pounds (4.3 billion kilograms).

No wonder, then, that New York City has the world's largest garbage dump. Named Fresh Kills, it is located on the western shore of Staten Island. Once, the 3,000-acre (7,400-hectare) site was marshland. Today, it is an ever-growing mountain.

More than 70% of the wastes entering the city's disposal system end up at Fresh Kills. Some arrives by truck. The rest arrives by barge. Garbage trucks that collect wastes in other parts of New York City take it to marine transfer stations. The trucks dump their loads onto barges. When the barges are full, they are pushed by tugboats to Fresh Kills. Huge cranes unload the wastes onto wagons. Tractors pull trains of garbage-filled wagons from the unloading plants up and up, to the active part of the landfill. Here the garbage reaches its final resting spot. It is dumped, bulldozed, sprayed with disinfectant, compacted and covered with a layer of soil.

Twenty-four hours a day, six days a week, barges are unloaded, tractor trains chug up the mountain and garbage is buried. But Fresh Kills is rapidly being filled. It may close before the end of the 1990s. When it closes, it will be one of the highest points on the east coast of North America. It will even be higher than the Washington Monument.

industries and greatly add to the piles of waste. People buy disposable razors rather than razors that last a lifetime. They drink juice from single-serving containers because it is more convenient than pouring juice from a large container into a glass. They gladly accept their fast-food hamburgers in plastic containers, use the containers for five minutes, then throw them into the environment, where they will remain for hundreds of years.

The Price Is High

For many people of the past and present, dumping wastes into the environment has been considered part of the price to be paid for growth, modernization and convenience. But the price of this pollution has been high.

Wastes dumped into the environment have killed and caused illness in untold millions of people. Some of the worst problems have resulted from drinking water or eating food polluted with human wastes. Hepatitis A, dysentery, typhoid and cholera are among the diseases spread in this manner. One cholera epidemic, which occurred in Russia in 1848, is thought to have killed a million people. Other wastes may be equally harmful to people's health, though their effects are slower to become apparent. Cancer-causing chemicals, or carcinogens, are common in many products of modern society, or in the wastes produced during the manufacture of these products. These chemicals enter the body as people breathe contaminated air, eat and drink contaminated food and water, and handle contaminated objects. Chemicals seem almost unavoidable. According to the U.S. Environmental Protection Agency (EPA), 90% of all Americans have measurable amounts of dioxins, benzene, dichlorobenzene, styrene and other suspected carcinogens in their body tissues.

Another price of wastes is the destruction of natural habitats and the plants and animals that depend on those habitats for their survival. Wetlands, which are important for the spawning of fish and shellfish, have been polluted by water from factories. Meadows where turtles and wild ducks once lived have been buried under mountains of trash. Ocean bottoms where lobsters crawled have been poisoned by sewage dumped from city treatment plants.

We pay an aesthetic price, too. No one wishes to live in an environment polluted with wastes. No joy comes from smelling a garbage dump, seeing litter on a woodland trail or finding medical wastes washed onto a beach.

Finally, we pay an economic price. Disposing of wastes is increasingly expensive. Cleaning up the messes created by mismanaged wastes is also expensive. In 1990, the EPA selected a cleanup plan for a 5,600-acre (2,270-hectare) site near Denver, Colorado, that was contaminated with hazardous wastes. The wastes included chromium solutions, rocket fuels and organic solvents dumped on the ground or buried in barrels during the 1970s. The plan calls for excavating the wastes and shipping it elsewhere to be incinerated. All the contaminated soil will be dug up, treated to remove contaminants, then put back on the ground. Groundwater will be pumped out and sent to a wastewater treatment plant to remove contaminants. The EPA has indicated that soil cleanup is expected to take 4 years; groundwater cleanup could take 45 years to complete. The estimated cost to clean up the site is $59 million. It is only one of thousands of contaminated sites in the United States. Similar sites are to be found almost everywhere on Earth.

Unfortunately, we do not even know the location of all these sites. Over the years, some were covered with soil, planted and sold as sites for homes and schools. Not until the wastes begin to seep to the surface, not until people in the area wonder why there is such a high incidence of cancer, will we perhaps discover the wastes.

No Easy Answers

Traditionally, people worried about wastes after they were created. Then the wastes were dumped into the environment, generally in some out-of-the-way place. "Out of sight, out of mind," was the philosophy.

But the wastes did not disappear. Today, many of them are creating serious problems. Not generating so many wastes in the first place would have been better. It would have avoided many problems that now threaten the environment and people's health.

Wherever, whenever, however possible, we should avoid creating wastes. This is called source reduction: limiting the amount of wastes by not producing them in the first place.

Source reduction saves valuable landfill and limits the need for incineration. It saves ores, fuels and other natural resources. It can also save money for individuals, businesses and communities. Over a 10-year period, 3M (Minnesota Mining and Manufacturing Company) cut the wastes it produced by 50%. It redesigned equipment, streamlined manufacturing processes and sold or reused materials that used to be discarded. As a result, it saved more than $300 million.

The next best alternative is recycling. This is the process of using something over and over again or of converting discarded materials into new products. Like source reduction, it saves natural resources and money, and it limits the production of wastes. If all Americans recycled all the used motor oil from their cars and trucks, the nation would save 1.3 million barrels of oil a day. If all Americans recycled all

IN SEARCH OF A PORT

Philadelphia, Pennsylvania, had a problem. Where could it dump the ash from its garbage incinerators? Tons of the stuff were piling up, forming an ever-growing mountain.

Disposal sites elsewhere in the United States refused to accept the ash. Then someone came up with an idea: let's export it!

The *Khian Sea*, a 17-year-old freighter, left Philadelphia in 1986. It carried nearly 15,000 tons of ash. It sailed south to the Bahamas, where the cargo was rejected. The Dominican Re-

public, Honduras and the West African nation of Guinea-Bissau didn't want the cargo. Then it appeared that an agreement to dump the ash had been reached with Panama. But the deal fell apart after the environmental group Greenpeace alerted Panamanians that the ash contained toxic heavy metals and chemicals.

The *Khian Sea* sailed on. Its owners twice changed its name, but this couldn't disguise the ship's cargo. For more than two years the *Khian Sea* looked in

vain for a place that would take Philadelphia's wastes. In November 1988, port officials in Singapore announced that the cargo had disappeared. No one would say where the ash had been dumped, though court documents later suggested it was dumped in the Indian Ocean.

This incident demonstrates the problems that arise as people create more wastes than their communities can handle. They don't want wastes in their own backyards. But no one else wants wastes, either.

---

their Sunday newspapers every week, the nation would save over 500,000 trees a year.

Source reduction and recycling are not possible for all materials. Even under ideal circumstances, people will continue to produce wastes. How should we dispose of these wastes? There are no easy answers to this question.

Pay as You Throw?

Regardless of which disposal method is used, waste disposal has become increasingly expensive. The price charged to dump garbage and other municipal wastes at a landfill or an incinerator is called a tipping fee. In the United States, the average tipping fee at a landfill was $10.80 in 1982. By 1988, it had more than doubled, reaching $26.93. The average tipping fee at an incinerator more than tripled, going from $12.91 in 1982 to $39.86 in 1988. Added to these costs are those needed to transport wastes to the landfills and incinerators, to clean up litter, to decontaminate old waste sites, to treat sewage and other wastewater, and so on.

Who should pay for all the wastes dumped into the environment? Should businesses, which pay for raw materials and manufacturing, also pay for disposal of the products they sell? Should the people who consume the products pay?

In most places, the costs are shared by all members of a community. Everyone's taxes are used to clean up an abandoned toxic waste site. Everyone's trash collection fees are identical.

Some communities are changing their policies, to reward citizens who are environmentally conscious and to place the financial burden on those who produce the wastes. In 1981, Seattle, Washington, introduced a policy that bases charges for trash collection on the number of standardized cans a household uses. As a result, the average number fell from 3.5 cans per week to just over one can per week.

Surcharges—charges or taxes on top of regular prices—are another tactic. In 1989, Florida imposed a 50-cent surcharge on each new tire sold—a fee that was raised to $1 in 1990. The money collected was used to finance disposal of worn-out tires.

Deposits on beverage containers and other items are also proving successful. "Requiring deposits on certain products and containers puts the cost of recycling or safe disposal where it belongs: on the consumer or the manufacturer, not the local government and everyone on the taxpayer rolls," explain Reid Lifset and Marian Chertow of the Project on Solid Waste and the Environment at Yale University.

Such tactics become increasingly important as communities run out of places to dump their wastes and as costs of waste disposal skyrocket. Instituting changes needs to be done now. The longer we wait to deal with our growing piles of wastes, the worse the problem will be. Finding solutions and changing life-styles may seem difficult. But they are tasks we cannot escape.

2

WHERE DOES IT COME FROM?

 A woman finishes her cigarette, then drops the butt on the sidewalk. A carful of people throw soda cans onto the roadside. A child drops a candy wrapper onto the ground. A man crumples an empty plastic coffee cup and tosses it into the woods. A boater dumps a plastic bag of trash into the sea.

Perhaps these people think, "So what? It's only one small item," or, "Someone will clean it up," or, "Lots of other people do it." But small items add up to create big amounts of litter—litter that makes the environment look ugly and that costs a great deal of money to clean up. Communities spend millions of dollars each year cleaning up this debris.

Pedestrians and motorists are usually blamed for litter. But Keep America Beautiful has identified five additional sources that contribute to the problem. They are commercial refuse sources, including dumpsters; household trash handling; construction and demolition sites; uncovered vehicles; and loading docks. Once the litter is dumped on the ground, says Keep America Beautiful, "it is carried in every direction by wind, water and traffic. It moves until trapped by a curb, wall, fence, a row of trees, a building or other stationary object. Once trapped, litter becomes not only an eyesore, but an invitation for people to add more."

Litter is highly visible. Yet it makes up only a tiny portion of our wastes.

Opposite page: Americans have become accustomed to the fancy, wasteful packaging of consumer goods. Heavy plastic wrappings and high-gloss coatings, while attractive to customers, are not biologically degradable and can remain unchanged in a landfill for hundreds of years.

Sources of Wastes

Quantities and composition of wastes vary among households, communities and nations. Many newspapers and magazines are purchased and discarded by one home but are rarely seen in a neighboring home. Yard wastes compose a larger percentage of the waste stream in Ingham County, Michigan, than in Atlantic County, New Jersey. Plastics make up a larger portion of residential wastes in the United States than they do in Europe.

There are seasonal variations, too. In warm weather, the number of beverage containers tends to rise. In autumn, leaves and other yard wastes increase in the American northeast.

Municipal Wastes

Solid wastes generated by people in their homes are called municipal solid wastes. Frequently, these wastes also include wastes from office buildings, stores and other businesses in a community.

In the United States, the amount of municipal wastes has grown continually through the years. It is expected to continue growing during the 1990s.

In addition to solid wastes, homes produce huge amounts of liquid wastes in the form of sewage.

Vehicular wastes include the millions of cars, buses and trucks that are scrapped each year, plus used oil, tires, batteries, oil filters and other items.

Medical Wastes

Hospitals, nursing homes, dental offices and other medical facilities create many of the same wastes created in homes. In addition, they create wastes that may be infectious. These include blood, syringes, needles, intravenous bags, urine bags, bandages, and body tissues from surgeries and autopsies.

Medical facilities also produce radioactive wastes. Radioactive materials are used to examine internal organs such as the brain, liver, kidneys and heart. They are also used to treat illnesses. For example, a radioactive form of iodine is used to

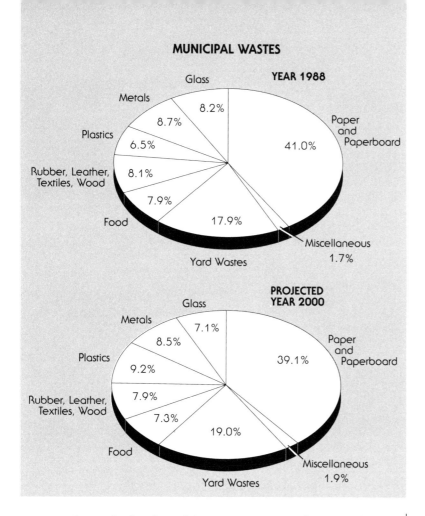

MUNICIPAL WASTES

YEAR 1988

- Glass 8.2%
- Metals 8.7%
- Plastics 6.5%
- Rubber, Leather, Textiles, Wood 8.1%
- Food 7.9%
- Yard Wastes 17.9%
- Miscellaneous 1.7%
- Paper and Paperboard 41.0%

PROJECTED YEAR 2000

- Glass 7.1%
- Metals 8.5%
- Plastics 9.2%
- Rubber, Leather, Textiles, Wood 7.9%
- Food 7.3%
- Yard Wastes 19.0%
- Miscellaneous 1.9%
- Paper and Paperboard 39.1%

treat a thyroid gland problem. During such procedures, syringes, containers, gloves and other items become contaminated by low levels of radioactivity.

Industrial Wastes

Materials discarded by factories, mines and other industrial operations are called industrial wastes. They include both solid and liquid wastes.

Each industry produces a unique mix of wastes. Mining operations produce huge piles of waste rocks, as well as water pollution. Lead smelters, petroleum refineries and battery manufacturers produce poisonous lead wastes. Paint manufacturers produce various metallic wastes.

Power plants that burn coal or oil to produce electricity produce massive amounts of carbon dioxide and other air pollutants. Power plants that use nuclear energy to produce

THE THROWAWAY SOCIETY

Each year Americans throw away 2 billion disposable razors and blades, 2 billion disposable ballpoint pens, 2.5 billion disposable batteries, 18 billion disposable diapers—plus billions of disposable flashlights, disposable plastic spoons and forks, disposable cigarette lighters and so on.

The throwaway mentality is wasteful. It wastes natural resources such as metals and petroleum. It wastes landfill space.

The throwaway mentality is environmentally harmful. It forces communities to cover natural habitats with garbage. If the wastes are burned, toxic chemicals are emitted into the air or left behind in ash that is discarded on land.

While some people enjoy short-term benefits from the throwaway mentality, everyone shares in the long-term costs. "Manufacturers profit from the sales of disposable goods; consumers benefit from the convenience; but the taxpayers who do not use these products are sharing the cost of this disposal," point out Reid Lifset and Marian Chertow of Yale University's Project on Solid Waste and the Environment.

"In the past, 'business as usual' meant an accelerating trend toward disposable products, convenience packaging, and an 'out-of-sight, out-of-mind' attitude toward solid waste. As a nation, we can no longer afford this kind of 'business as usual,'" stressed J. Winston Porter, Assistant Administrator of the U.S. Environmental Protection Agency's Solid Waste and Emergency Response.

electricity produce radioactive wastes. Weapons production and nuclear research also produce radioactive wastes.

Farms produce chemical wastes such as pesticides and fertilizers. Manure comes from cattle feedlots. When crops are harvested, there are plant wastes such as straws, hulls and bagasse (the dry pulp remaining from sugar cane after the juice has been extracted). Bones, blood and feathers come from slaughtered animals. Millions of gallons of wastewater containing large amounts of minerals and organic matter come from processing canned and frozen fruits and vegetables. There are outdated bakery and dairy products and new cereals and other consumer products that do not sell.

American industries use some 70,000 different chemicals. Hundreds of new chemicals are added to the list every year. Many of these chemicals end up in wastewater, or effluent, that is discharged into rivers and other waters. Others end up in air emissions or solid wastes. Still more chemical compounds are formed during production processes. For example, pulp and paper mills use chlorine to bleach pulp, in order to produce white paper. In the process, a hazardous waste called dioxin is formed.

Plastics

The fastest growing segment of the waste stream is composed of plastics. In 1970, plastics made up only 2.7% of U.S. municipal wastes; by 1990, they made up about 7%.

In the United States alone, some 60 billion pounds (27 billion kilograms) of plastics are produced annually. Many of them are molded into packaging, disposable eating utensils and other items that soon become part of the waste stream.

Plastics have thousands of uses because they are durable, flexible and long-lasting. The latter characteristic is an advantage during the useful life of a plastic item, but a disadvantage once the item is discarded. The item can remain unchanged in the environment for hundreds of years. Another problem is that many of the chemicals used to manufacture plastics and plastic items are highly toxic. These include propylene, phenol, ethylene, styrene and benzene.

The basic raw material of today's plastics is petroleum. It is turned into many different kinds of plastics. One of the most common kinds is polyethylene terephthalate (PET), which is lightweight, transparent and resistant to moisture. It is widely used to bottle soft drinks.

Polypropylene (PP) is used for yogurt containers, butter and margarine containers, syrup bottles and containers for some detergents, shampoos and medicines.

Polyvinyl chloride (PVC) is used for detergent bottles, oil bottles and plastic wrap. Almost all packaged meats are wrapped in PVC, which keeps the meats from turning brown.

There are two types of polyethylene (PE). Low-density polyethylene (LDPE) is used as a food wrap. It is also used to make supermarket produce bags, bread bags and garment bags. High-density polyethylene (HDPE) is stronger than LDPE. It is used to make plastic milk bottles, bleach and detergent bottles, containers for ice cream and cosmetics, heavy-duty trash bags and the base cups of PET soft-drink bottles.

There also are two basic types of polystyrene (PS). Crystal PS is used to make clear plastic cups and deli containers. Foam PS is used to make disposable dishes and cups, fast-food containers called clamshells and packing material. This

BEACH SWEEP

In 1989, Peg Van Patten of the University of Connecticut's Sea Grant Program organized a Beach Sweep along the Connecticut shore. More than 550 people volunteered to pick up trash. In just one day, these people picked up three tons of garbage from 58 miles (93 kilometers) of beach!

Plastic made up 62% of the wastes. There were 3,982 plastic eating utensils, 1,343 plastic lids, 1,202 plastic bags, 979 plastic bottles, 1,574 polystyrene cups, 2,430 pieces of plastic foam and 2,444 other plastic pieces. There were 3,300 glass pieces, 2,118 cigarette butts, 1,977 pieces of paper, 1,350 metal beverage cans and 799 metal bottle caps.

The trash included 24 drums (each 55-gallons/208-liters), 6 syringes, fishing and boating gear, two dozen tires, a refrigerator, two washing machines and a car transmission.

THE JUNKYARD IN SPACE

High above the Earth's surface is a giant junkyard. There are no soda cans, wrappers from fast-food restaurants or worn out tires in this junkyard. Instead, it contains nonfunctioning satellites, burned-out rocket stages and other items sent into space by people. Some of the satellites and rockets have exploded or broken into tiny pieces that can cause serious problems.

No one knows exactly how many items are orbiting the Earth. Some experts estimate that there are as many as 70,000 bits of debris 0.4 inch (1 centimeter) or larger in diameter. Most of this space junk orbits the Earth at relatively low altitudes—about 300 to 500 miles (480 to 800 kilometers) above the Earth. But some is more than 22,000 miles (35,200 kilometers) up.

Space junk is messy. Astronomers complain about its presence. Sunlight reflecting off the junk's surfaces is picked up by telescopes, thereby interfering with astronomers' observations of the universe.

Space junk is also potentially dangerous. Some pieces zip along at very high speeds. If they collide with a spacecraft, they can cause a great deal of damage. For instance, a particle the size of a grain of sand, moving at a speed of several thousand miles per hour, would have enough force to penetrate the shell of a space shuttle. This could cause the astronauts' cabin to lose its pressure and oxygen.

No manned spacecraft has ever experienced such a catastrophic collision. However, in 1983 a tiny paint chip collided with the window of the space shuttle *Challenger*. It damaged the window so badly that the window had to be replaced. Fast-moving space junk may also have been responsible for destroying satellites that unexpectedly exploded.

By 1990, the U.S. military was tracking 6,645 objects that were 4 inches (10 centimeters) or more in diameter. Four inches is about the size of a softball. A report by the U.S. Congressional Office of Technology Assess-

ment warned that countries had to reduce the amount of space junk they generated. Otherwise, shuttle flights and other space activity could become too risky. "Continuing steady growth of orbital debris could, by 2000 or 2010, render some well-used, low-Earth orbits too risky to use," the report said.

Space scientists are studying ways to protect spacecraft from the debris. One defense may be the Whipple shield, named for British astronomer Fred Whipple, who suggested it. The shield would consist of two or more layers of lightweight material, with spaces between the layers. It would be placed over critical parts of a space station. It is estimated that the Whipple shield would break up about 80% of the small items that collided with it. What wasn't broken up, would at least be deflected.

Another defense might be a laser gun. If the astronomers saw a piece of debris headed toward their vehicle, it could be destroyed with a laser beam before it ever collided with anything.

---

plastic is better known by the Dow company's trade name Styrofoam.

Multi-resin, or multi-plastic, containers are composed of several layers of different plastics. One layer may protect flavor, another may provide strength, and so on. There may be as many as 10 layers. Squeezable bottles for jelly, jam, ketchup and margarine are multi-resin items.

Air Pollution

In addition to dumping wastes onto land and into waterways, human activities emit hundreds of millions of tons of wastes into the air each year. The major source of these wastes varies from country to country. In the United States and Canada, it is transportation: the burning of fossil fuels to operate cars, trucks, buses and other vehicles. In eastern Europe, power plants and factories are the major sources. In rural Africa, indoor cooking and heating fires are the biggest problem.

The air pollutants produced by these activities harm the environment in many ways. Some, such as carbon dioxide and methane, are causing the Earth's temperatures to rise, in a phenomenon known as the *greenhouse effect*. Some, particularly chlorofluorocarbons (CFCs), are destroying the atmosphere's ozone layer, which protects the Earth from harmful radiation. Some form acids that damage lakes and forests. And some damage human health.

"In this part of the world, nobody takes breathing for granted," commented Olga Banlaky, an elderly citizen of Budapest, Hungary. The countries of eastern Europe are living with—and dying from—some of the worst air pollution on Earth. This is a legacy of many years of industry without air pollution controls. Factories operating 24 hours a day spewed out thick coal-based clouds that darkened the sky and covered everything with soot.

Even countries with comparatively strict air quality control standards have serious air pollution problems. In 1989, the U.S. Environmental Protection Agency reported that the nation's industries pour more than 2.6 billion pounds (1.8 billion kilograms) of toxic wastes into the skies each year: more than 10 pounds (4.5 kilograms) for each person living in the country. "The magnitude of this problem far exceeds our worst fears," commented U.S. Representative Henry Waxman of California.

In places like Southern California, which has the United States' dirtiest air, gasoline-fueled vehicles create much of the problem. The problem is quickly apparent, for visibility is frequently limited by a dirty mixture of smoke and fog called smog. But no part of the nation—indeed, no part of the world—is immune to air pollution.

3

WHERE DOES IT GO?

Until recently, people did not think much about the wastes they produced in their homes: kitchen scraps, empty boxes and cans, newspapers, lawn clippings, torn clothing, rags, crumpled gift wrap, soiled cat litter, worn-out batteries, broken glass, scraps of metal. These and other unwanted items were placed in plastic bags or large garbage cans. In some places, people took these to the town dump. Elsewhere, people set the wastes outdoors, where a trash collector picked them up and hauled them away.

Most people call the wastes garbage. Government officials call them municipal solid wastes. The United States has the dubious distinction of leading the world in producing municipal solid wastes. Americans produce more such waste per capita than any other nation. Each person contributes an average of 3.6 pounds (1.6 kilograms) a day, or 1,300 pounds (590 kilograms) a year. The nation as a whole produces more than 160 million tons of the stuff each year. This is enough to fill a convoy of 10-ton garbage trucks some 145,000 miles (232,000 kilometers) long.

By the year 2000, Americans are expected to generate 190 million tons of garbage a year. Where will they put the stuff?

Like other countries, America traditionally disposed of garbage in open dumps and gulleys. This marred the natural beauty of an area. It attracted rats and other vermin. And the odors from rotting items were sometimes overpowering.

Opposite page: Shredded burnable garbage moves from its holding bin to the boiler hoppers at a garbage-burning power plant in Columbus, Ohio.

In the 1930s, the first sanitary landfills were established in the United States. Several decades later, some communities were running out of room. They were unable to find enough sites for new landfills. They began to burn wastes in special incinerators. By the beginning of the 1990s, Americans were disposing of about 80% of their garbage in landfills. About 10% of the nation's garbage was handled by incinerators. The remaining 10% was recycled.

Sanitary Landfills

The open dumps of the past have been replaced by much safer disposal sites called sanitary landfills. Here, municipal wastes are spread in layers and sometimes sprayed with disinfectants.

Huge bulldozers compact the wastes, reducing them to the smallest practical volume. At the end of each day, or often more frequently, the wastes are covered with a layer of soil. This, too, is compacted. Compaction limits wind-blown litter. It also helps control insects and rodents.

When the site cannot hold any more wastes, it is capped with a material such as clay or plastic. These materials are not very permeable. They prevent or severely limit the ability of rainwater to seep into the wastes. A layer of soil, usually about 2 feet (0.6 meter) thick, is added on top of the cap. Grass and other vegetation is planted in the soil.

Sometimes, closed landfills are used as parks, golf courses or ski slopes. In New York City, there are more than 250 reclaimed landfills. They include many parks, of which the most famous is Flushing Meadow Park, where the 1939–1940 and 1964–1965 World Fairs were held. Parts of the city's La Guardia and Kennedy International airports are built on landfill. City highways run atop landfills. Riker's Island, which houses a city prison, consists mainly of landfill.

A major concern connected to landfills is leachate. This consists of water that trickles through the wastes, picking up dissolved or suspended contaminants. The contaminants— primarily toxic chemicals and metals—come from household hazardous wastes and other materials dumped in the landfill. If the leachate is not stopped, it can contaminate groundwater and surface water. Cleaning up such contamination can be very costly. This is a serious problem around many older landfills.

A state-of-the-art landfill has safeguards to protect against contamination of the surrounding environment. An impermeable liner at the base of the landfill, made of clay or plastic, prevents leachate from seeping into the ground. Sometimes, more than one liner is used. Pipes at the bottom of the landfill collect the leachate, which can then be removed and treated. At the landfill's boundaries, monitors are installed to detect any hazardous releases and changes in nearby groundwater.

In the United States, landfills must be monitored and maintained for at least 20 years after they are closed. Environmentalists worry about what happens after those 20 years. They point out that some of the plastic liners used in new landfills have already developed leaks during the years of operation.

Certain municipal wastes present unique problems. Disposing of them in municipal landfills is—or should be—prohibited. For example, household wastes such as paints, solvents, pesticides and used oil are poisonous. They should be disposed of in a special manner rather than mixed in with regular household wastes or poured down a storm sewer.

At the beginning of the 1990s, approximately 10,000 landfills were operating in the United States. Many of these

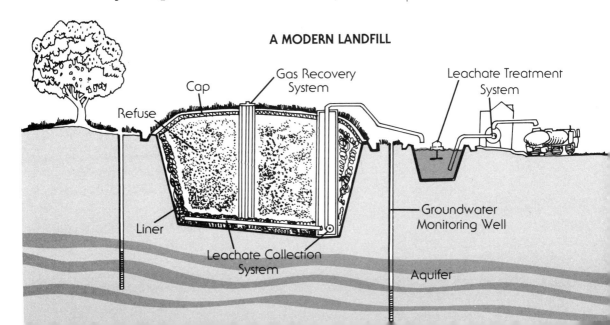

A MODERN LANDFILL

Cap · Gas Recovery System · Leachate Treatment System · Refuse · Liner · Leachate Collection System · Groundwater Monitoring Well · Aquifer

facilities were built and operated prior to the introduction of strict environmental regulations. They do not meet current standards. Many are unlined and contain toxic wastes, thereby presenting costly cleanup problems.

As local landfills have reached capacity, communities have had to find other places to dump their garbage. This has led to shipping wastes by trucks and railroads to distant communities where private landfill operators are willing to sell some of their available capacity. Heidelberg, Germany, has transported wastes to France for landfilling. Other cities in western Germany shipped their garbage to eastern Germany, prior to the unification of the two areas.

In the United States, shipping garbage has been particularly common in the Northeast, where the fees charged by landfills to unload garbage are highest. By the late 1980s, as disposal costs skyrocketed at scarce New Jersey landfills, many towns found it was cheaper to truck garbage 400 miles (644 kilometers) to Ohio than to bury it in the state.

People in communities that received imported wastes have become increasingly vocal in their opposition to "someone else's garbage." Among their concerns was the loss of landfill space that would be needed for their own wastes. "We can't handle New Jersey's problems and still plan rationally for our own solid waste needs," explained Richard Sahli, chairman of Ohio's Solid Waste Management Advisory Council. Between 1971 and 1991, the number of open landfills in Ohio declined from 360 to less than 130.

Legislation has been enacted in some places to exclude, limit or otherwise regulate waste imports. In other instances, public opposition has forced town officials to back out of deals they made to accept outsiders' garbage. One highly publicized incident occurred in 1987, when Morehead, North Carolina, officials turned away the *Mobro*. This garbage scow was laden with 3,186 tons of wastes from Islip, New York. After it was rejected by Morehead, the *Mobro* tried to dump the wastes somewhere else. It wasn't successful. Five more states and three nations along the Atlantic coast and Gulf of Mexico also refused to accept the *Mobro*'s load. Finally, the barge returned to New York and the garbage was burned.

Incineration

Burning garbage in special incinerators has gained popularity because it can reduce the volume of wastes by up to 90%. The ash that remains must be landfilled, but it takes up much less space than the original garbage.

Two types of combustion facilities are most common. Mass burn systems burn municipal wastes with very little preprocessing. Only a few items, such as scrap tires and items that are too large to be fed into the unit, need to be removed. Refuse-derived fuel facilities remove toxic materials plus recyclable materials such as glass and metals. The remaining materials are shredded to produce small fuel particles that are relatively uniform in size.

Incinerators are expensive to build. A large incinerator that can burn 3,000 tons or more of garbage can cost as much as $250 million to build. They may also be difficult to operate, particularly if restricted wastes inadvertently enter the plant. In 1984, an explosion at an incinerator in Akron, Ohio, killed three workers, injured seven others and caused an estimated $1 million in damage. Apparently, highly flammable paint thinners were in the garbage.

A major disadvantage of incinerators is the risk of pollution. Air emissions may contain a variety of dangerous substances. These include unburned particles called fly ash, heavy metals, acid gases (sulfur oxides, hydrogen chloride, hydrogen fluoride), dioxins and nitrogen oxides. Some of the chemicals enter the plant in the garbage. Others are formed during the burning process or while the gases are moving upward through the smokestacks.

Proponents of incineration claim that production of toxic pollutants can be minimized by burning the wastes at very high temperatures. Also, they say that scrubbers, filters and other equipment can collect as much as 99% of any toxic air emissions that are produced. However, many incinerators operate without sufficient monitoring of temperatures in the combustion chamber. Also, many do not have BACT. BACT stands for "best available control technology." It refers to the best methods and equipment that are available to limit emissions.

In addition to air emissions, an incinerator produces wastes called bottom ash. These materials collect at the bottom of the combustion chamber. Bottom ash must be cooled and removed. It contains toxic metals, especially lead and cadmium, which are present in such materials as lead-acid batteries, electronic equipment and some plastics.

Frequently, the fly ash from the smokestack and the bottom ash from the combustion chamber are mixed together and transported to a landfill. There is considerable opposition to this practice. Fly ash consists of smaller particles than bottom ash. Thus it has proportionally more surface area on which pollutants can stick. As a result, it contains much higher concentrations of toxic substances. Environmentalists believe that fly ash should be disposed of in a hazardous waste landfill, where special liners help protect against the possibility of leaching.

Garbage In, Fuel Out

Many garbage-burning incinerators are waste-to-energy plants. The heat produced during the burning process is used to boil water. The resulting steam goes to a turbine-generator, which produces electricity. Generally, the plant uses some of the energy to operate fans and other equipment. The rest is sold. Money obtained from the sale of energy can help reduce an incinerator's operating costs.

Each ton of garbage burned produces about 500 kilowatt-hours of electricity. This is the amount used by a typical home in a month. In Columbus, Ohio, a facility that burns 2,000 tons of garbage a day generates 50,000 kilowatts of electricity per hour. In Baltimore, Maryland, a waste-to-energy plant that burns 2,250 tons of garbage a day produces steam that helps heat 500 office buildings, plus electricity that is sold to a local utility.

A number of waste-to-energy plants in the United States have had operating difficulties. One problem with early plants built during the 1960s and 1970s was that they were based on European technology. But American garbage is different than European garbage. It contains much more plastic and toxic metal, which produce dangerous emissions.

In 1989, the nation's largest waste-to-energy incinerator began operations in Detroit, Michigan, burning up to 3,300 tons of garbage a day. Less than a year later, state officials shut it down. They said that mercury emissions were higher than permitted by state law. The incinerator was back in service two weeks later. But Detroit had to agree to install scrubbers, which had not been required when the facility was originally approved. It also agreed to reduce the amount of wastes that contained high concentrations of mercury, such as small household batteries.

Energy can also be obtained from landfills. In a landfill, billions of microorganisms eat the decomposing garbage. In the process, they produce methane gas. If sufficient quantities are produced, the methane can be extracted and used for energy.

A deep hole is drilled into the landfill. A perforated pipe is inserted into the hole. Gas seeps from the landfill into the pipe. Periodically, a valve atop the pipe is opened to collect the methane.

Hundreds of companies in the United States capture methane from both inactive and active landfills. In New York City, the Brooklyn Union Gas Company uses methane produced at the city's Fresh Kills landfill to provide heating and cooking gas to 10,000 families.

The amount of methane produced within a landfill is often limited by the rate of decomposition. The process is slowed because the microorganisms do not have sufficient water. "Lack of moisture is a major reason that undecayed refuse 20 to 30 years old can be found in landfills today," said geologist Jean Bogner of Argonne National Laboratory in Illinois. Research conducted by Bogner indicates that circulating water through landfills could triple the speed of decomposition. This would increase production of methane gas.

An Integrated Approach

Handling and disposing of wastes is expensive. In addition, even when properly designed and managed, landfills and incinerators create potential threats to human health and the environment. What are the alternatives?

Many experts believe that the best approach to managing municipal solid wastes is a system called integrated waste management. This system involves the use of four practices: source reduction, recycling, combustion and landfills. Until now, the emphasis has been on landfills and incinerators. To solve the waste crisis, a major shift toward source reduction and recycling is essential.

Source reduction means reducing both the amount of waste and its toxicity. This may be done during the design and manufacture of products by changing packaging, and by making products that last longer. All segments of a society—including governments, manufacturers and consumers—are responsible for source reduction. For example, by redesigning products to contain less lead and cadmium, manufacturers reduce the risks of toxic chemicals going into landfills or out of smokestacks. By drinking water from glasses rather than paper cups, consumers will generate less garbage. (See Chapter 9.)

Recycling converts useful materials into new products. Like reduction, this diverts wastes from landfills and incinerators, reduces risks to health and the environment, and conserves energy and other natural resources. Governments can provide economic incentives for recycling materials. Manufacturers can make products from recycled materials and make products that can be recycled. Similarly, consumers can purchase products made from recycled materials—and from materials that can be recycled. (See Chapter 10.)

Even the most effective reduction and recycling efforts cannot handle all wastes. Some wastes have to be discarded. Because of their potential risks, however, incinerators and landfills should be used only when necessary. They need to be well constructed and maintained. Strict pollution controls are needed. And in many places, better training must be provided to landfill and incinerator operators.

Of the 160 million tons of municipal wastes generated each year in the United States, the Environmental Protection Agency (EPA) estimates that 3.2 million tons are medical wastes from hospitals. Much of this is paper and other harmless refuse. An estimated 10% to 15%, however, is potentially infectious. This includes human blood and blood products, wastes from surgeries and autopsies, wastes from patients isolated with highly communicable diseases, used needles, scalpels and other sharp items.

In addition to hospitals, there are numerous other sources of these wastes. These include private medical and dental practices, veterinary clinics, laboratories, blood banks and home health care activities. Many of these produce only small quantities of wastes.

The risk of contracting diseases from exposure to medical wastes is considered to be very low. Nonetheless, the wastes should be handled in such a way that exposure is prevented.

Recycling is not an acceptable option for infectious wastes. Incineration appears to be the best solution. Most hospitals burn medical wastes in on-site incinerators. EPA data indicates that 70% of hospital wastes in the United States is treated in this manner. Another 15% is sterilized in steam-heated vessels called autoclaves. This kills microorganisms in the wastes, so that the wastes can be placed in landfills. The remaining 15% is transported off-site for treatment. Before these wastes leave the hospital, they must be packed securely in leak-resistant containers.

Many hospital incinerators began operating before strict air pollution controls were established. They also operate at temperatures too low to completely burn the chlorinated plastics used in disposable instruments, intravenous tubing, syringes and other items. As a result, the incinerators emit some extremely hazardous substances into the air.

Outside medical institutions each year, Americans use over one billion needles, syringes and other sharp objects in their homes to administer health care. These items should be disposed of in hard plastic or metal containers that have screw-on or another type of tightly secured lid.

Soiled bandages and dressings, disposable sheets, medical gloves and other contaminated materials should also be disposed of carefully. The EPA recommends that they be placed in securely fastened plastic bags before they are put in the garbage can with other trash.

The chemical industry tried to stop the book's publication. Some people suggested the book was part of a sinister communist plot. Its writer was vilified and condemned. But *Silent Spring* was published, and it helped change the world.

Silent Spring, by the American writer Rachel Carson, was published in 1962. In it, Carson criticized the indiscriminate use of pesticides. She described the dangers to human health of chemicals such as the insecticide malathion and the weed killer 2,4-D (2,4-dichlorophenoxyacetic acid). The resulting controversy led to increased research on the effects of pesticides. It sparked public awareness of the hidden costs of many chemicals. And it accelerated the growth of the environmental movement.

Another pesticide that Carson warned against was DDT (dichlorodiphenyltrichloroethane). First used as an insecticide during World War II, DDT was extremely effective against mosquitoes. It was responsible for eliminating malaria and yellow fever, both transmitted by mosquitoes, as major diseases in the United States and other countries.

Carson presented evidence that DDT was also responsible for the drastic reduction of many bird populations. The result, she wrote, was that "over increasingly large areas of the United States, spring now comes unheralded by the return of the birds, and the early mornings are strangely silent where once they were filled with the beauty of bird song."

Opposite page:
Of the more than 66,000 chemicals legally used in the United States today, 60,000 are classified by the Environmental Protection Agency as hazardous or potentially hazardous.

DDT residues were being concentrated in habitats and organisms, including species that lived far from places that were being sprayed with the chemical. Scientists detected significant amounts of DDT in Adélie penguins from Antarctica, in bluefin tuna caught off Central America, and in open-ocean birds such as the Bermuda cahow, which comes on land only once a year to breed. In a marsh on Long Island, New York, that had been heavily sprayed with DDT, concentrations of the pesticide in the soil were as high as 32 pounds per acre (36 kilograms per hectare)!

DDT is fatal to birds at certain concentrations. It also interferes with reproduction. It causes birds to lay eggs with very thin shells that break before hatching.

By 1972, pressure from environmentalists resulted in the banning of most uses of DDT in the United States. But certain uses continued. Also, the country continued to export DDT to other countries. Some of this DDT returns to Americans, as contamination on foods that they import.

Malathion and 2,4-D continue to be used in massive quantities, even in the United States. The same is true for other toxic chemicals mentioned by Carson plus numerous additional chemicals that subsequent research has determined are dangerous.

A significant percentage of these chemicals end up as wastes. In 1987, U.S. industries produced more than 10.3 billion pounds (4.7 billion kilograms) of toxic wastes. Additional toxic wastes were produced as people threw half-used containers of pesticides and paints into garbage cans. More resulted as people splashed wood preservatives on the ground, poured drain cleaners down pipes and spilled antifreeze on driveways. Still more were produced by the military, service stations and homeowners during routine maintenance of cars and other vehicles.

Poisoning the World

More than 66,000 different chemicals are used regularly in the United States. Of these, 60,000 have been classified by

THE WASTE CRISIS
The Problems

Available space in America's valuable landfills is rapidly shrinking.

PEOPLE, PARTICULARLY IN INDUSTRIALIZED NATIONS, create enormous amounts of garbage. The United States leads the world on a per capita basis, producing more than 160 million tons of the stuff each year. All the food scraps, empty boxes and cans, newspapers, broken glass, worn-out batteries, scraps of metal, garden debris, discarded automobiles and other unwanted items must be put somewhere. Traditionally, most have ended up in sanitary landfills or open dumps. This destroys natural habitats and frequently contaminates the surrounding environment. Additional problems arise as communities run out of space to dump their garbage, and as the costs of waste disposal skyrocket. Yet people continue to produce—and discard—more and more garbage.

Left: A sea of abandoned cars awaits compacting at a junkyard in New Jersey.

FACTORIES, SMELTERS, MINES, PETROLEUM REFINERIES and other industrial operations produce large quantities of wastes. Thousands of chemicals, many of them toxic, end up in wastewater discharged into rivers and other waters. Other chemicals are emitted into the atmosphere or discarded as solid or liquid wastes. Large quantities of industrial wastes are improperly discarded, contaminating water supplies, soil and air. This creates health hazards to humans and other living organisms.

Left: Slag is heated to extremely high temperatures before it is recycled for later use. *Above:* Oil spills around the world kill marine wildlife populations and can make environments uninhabitable for decades to come.

Below: A Missouri farmer sprays his crops. *Right:* Workers from the Environmental Protection Agency clean up hazardous waste left behind by a paint manufacturer that went bankrupt.

HAZARDOUS AND RADIOACTIVE WASTES CREATE PARTICULAR PROBLEMS because of their harmful effects on living things. Some pesticides used by farmers contain chemicals that kill helpful insects and birds. Bandages, used scalpels and other wastes discarded by hospitals are often contaminated with infectious germs. Heavy metals, most of which are carcinogens, are used in the manufacture of everything from paints and camera batteries to gasoline and automobile tires. The nuclear power industry and nuclear weapons plants produce wastes that remain radioactive—and thus a threat to living cells—for centuries.

USING OCEANS AS DUMPING GROUNDS for wastes creates numerous problems. Sewage poisons or buries bottom-dwelling marine life, including economically valuable fish. Oil from flushed ship holds coats bird feathers, causing the birds to freeze to death. Broken fishing nets entangle and drown dolphins. Many wastes are eventually washed ashore, killing beach organisms, creating health hazards and ruining business in seaside resorts.

Below: Trash washes up on the shores of a northern Pacific beach.

A-B-C-D-BUTTON

Shopping list: AA cells for the portable radio, D cells for the flashlight and a "button" for the camera. Take these batteries home, remove and discard the used batteries, insert the new ones. Quick, easy and deadly.

Household batteries contain such toxic substances as mercury, zinc, cadmium, silver and nickel. When discarded in landfills, the batteries corrode and the metals leach into the ground, possibly contaminating groundwater. When the batteries are incinerated, the toxic metals contaminate fly ash and bottom ash, which generally are discarded in landfills.

Because billions of household batteries are used each year, the amount of pollution is considerable. Studies in Canada and Sweden found that batteries were the principal source of mercury emissions in those countries. In the United States,

lead-acid batteries contributed approximately 65% of the lead in municipal solid wastes. Nickel-cadmium batteries are the number one contributor of cadmium in municipal solid wastes.

Batteries can be recycled instead of discarded. This is commonly done in Europe and Japan. For example, Sweden and Switzerland have collection

centers for batteries from portable radios, cameras, hearing aids and other products. In 1987, Bornholm, Denmark, became the first community in the world to put a surcharge on batteries. The money is refunded when the consumer returns the used batteries.

In the United States, recycling is only beginning to catch on. However, one U.S. firm, Mercury Refining Company of Latham, New York, has been reclaiming mercury and silver from batteries since the 1950s. It helps communities set up battery recycling programs.

Another alternative is to use nickel-cadmium rechargeable batteries. Their initial cost is more, and they require the purchase of a recharger. But most such batteries can be recharged as many as 1,000 times. Then, the nickel and cadmium can be reclaimed and reused.

the U.S. Environmental Protection Agency as being hazardous or potentially hazardous.

These chemicals are hazardous because of their effects on living things. They cause disease and death in humans and other organisms. Some are teratogens: they injure developing embryos, causing birth defects. Some are mutagens: they damage chromosomes, which can result in genetic changes in subsequent generations.

When they enter the environment, hazardous chemicals make habitats unfit for plants and animals. They also make land and water unusable for human activities. Land contaminated with hazardous wastes cannot be used for houses or playgrounds. Groundwater and surface waters contaminated with these wastes cannot be used as drinking water supplies.

Many hazardous chemicals can accumulate in food chains. Like DDT, they are easily absorbed and retained in the tissues of living organisms, thereby presenting long-term dangers.

Some chemicals are hazardous in extremely small concentrations. One type of dioxin, among the most toxic of all chemicals, will kill small freshwater fish called mosquito minnow at concentrations of three parts per trillion parts of water.

Other chemicals are known to be hazardous in high concentrations. Little is known, however, about the effects of low-level, long-term, cumulative exposure to these substances. "Too many substances and compounds are entering our homes, our working place, our environment and our bodies without our really knowing their risks and benefits, without a true evaluation of their usefulness and—worse still—without complete studies of their harmlessness for other forms of life," noted Jenny Pronczuk de Garbino, associate professor of clinical toxicology at the Universidad de la República in Uruguay.

Types of Hazardous Wastes

Wastes that are flammable, corrosive, chemically reactive or toxic are considered hazardous wastes. Radioactive wastes, while certainly hazardous, are generally considered to be a separate category of wastes.

Flammable chemicals react with oxygen, giving off enormous amounts of heat in the process. Petroleum and natural gas by-products are the most common flammables.

Strong acids and bases can cause a great deal of damage by corroding metals, stone and even living tissues. For example, concentrated acids or bases released into a lake or stream can be lethal to fish and other aquatic organisms. Another problem is that acids in particular are very reactive. They can dissolve heavy metals present in soils, carrying them into groundwater and surface water supplies.

Heavy metals, asbestos and halogenated hydrocarbons such as DDT are among the most serious toxic wastes.

CENSORED ART?

Paints, solvents, glues and other materials commonly used by artists can be hazardous. Many can cause allergic skin reactions and respiratory ailments. Some can cause cancer. But suggest banning these substances and you have a fight on your hands.

In 1989, U.S. Senator John Chafee of Rhode Island proposed an amendment to the Solid Waste Disposal Act. Its purpose was to limit the amount of toxic substances entering the waste stream. The amendment would ban, among other things, the use of cadmium as a pigment and the importation of products containing cadmium as a pigment.

When artists learned about the amendment, they put down their paintbrushes and picked up their pens: "During this Con-

gress I have received more mail on this issue than on any other hazardous waste issue facing the American public," said Senator Quentin N. Burdick of North Dakota, chairman of the Environment and Public Works Committee.

Cadmium is used to produce extremely vivid paints. Banning it, say artists, would limit the range of their expression. "Losing cadmiums would be like a composer losing the use of several keys," commented painter Robert Cottingham.

By the time the issue comes up for a vote in Congress, an exception to the cadmium ban may be made for artists' pigments. Is this fair? Other cadmium users may feel that they also deserve to be exempted. Should exceptions to the ban be made for them, too? Can exemptions be made without destroying the purpose of the amendment?

Some environmentalists say the issue is simple: who has the right to pollute the environment?

Heavy Metals

Metallic elements with large molecules are called heavy metals. They include arsenic, beryllium, cadmium, chromium, copper, lead, mercury and zinc.

Industry has many uses for heavy metals. Lead, for example, is used in piping, paints and gasoline. Mercury is used in paints, batteries and the manufacture of chlorine. It also is a common drug ingredient. Cadmium is used in the electroplating industry, to make protective coatings for metals that are vulnerable to corrosion. It is used in many batteries and paint pigments. It also is present in motor vehicle tires; as the treads wear down, cadmium is released onto streets. When it rains, cadmium washes into sewers.

Most heavy metals are carcinogens. Many cause other health problems. Lead damages nerves and causes learning disabilities. Mercury also damages nerves and can cause skin rashes. Cadmium has been linked to high blood pressure, kidney damage, lung and prostate cancer and reproductive disorders.

Asbestos

Asbestos is the name given to a group of minerals composed of thin, threadlike fibers. Asbestos is durable; that is, it can withstand a lot of wear and tear. It also is very resistant to heat, fire and corrosion. These qualities have made asbestos very useful. More than 3,000 products in use today contain asbestos. It has been used for insulation, fireproofing, roofing and flooring materials, patching and spackling compounds, ironing board pads, and in friction products such as automobile brake linings.

Asbestos becomes dangerous when it ages or is disturbed. It crumbles, releasing fibers into the air. The most dangerous fibers are too small to be visible. They can remain suspended in the air for a long time, and they are easily inhaled. Once in the lungs, they are likely to remain, penetrating and irritating the lung cells.

Asbestos can cause lung cancer and mesothelioma, a cancer of the chest and abdominal linings. It also causes asbestosis, a scarring of the lungs that makes breathing difficult. Symptoms of these diseases do not show up until many years after exposure began.

As long ago as the first century A.D., the Roman naturalist Pliny the Elder pointed out the health hazards of asbestos. In more recent times, British scientists reported as early as 1907 that exposure to asbestos can cause the disease now called asbestosis. By 1918, American insurance companies considered asbestos workers to be poor risks because of their very high death rates. In the 1930s, studies in Britain found high rates of asbestosis and lung cancer in asbestos textile workers.

The asbestos industry made no effort to publicize the data. Indeed, quite the opposite was true. In 1935, the president of one asbestos firm, Raybestos-Manhattan, wrote to the lawyer for Johns-Mansville Corp., the largest asbestos producer in the United States: "I think the less said about asbestos, the better off we are." To which the lawyer replied: "I quite agree

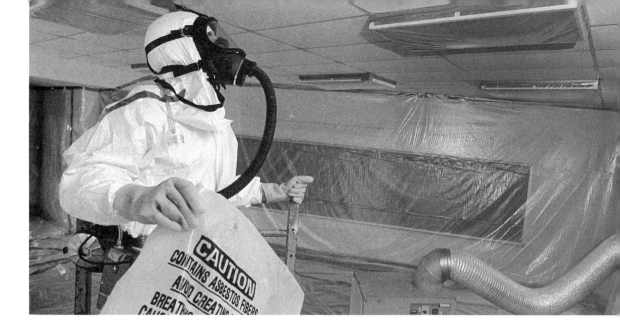

with you that our interests are best served by having asbestosis receive the minimum of publicity."

As a result, it is estimated that since 1940 as many as 11 million American workers have been subjected to excessive exposure to asbestos. The largest group were the 4.5 million men and women who worked in U.S. shipyards during and immediately after World War II. It was not unusual for them to finish a workday completely covered in asbestos dust. Many of these people never reached old age. Among those who did, many spent their last days fighting to breathe.

Many buildings constructed between 1950 and 1970 had asbestos sprayed onto ceilings, walls, and pipes for insulation. A large number of carpenters, electricians, steamfitters and other construction workers were exposed to the asbestos. Because of the long latency period of the lung diseases, the effects on these workers is only now becoming apparent.

During the 1970s, the United States started to take action to limit exposure to asbestos. It also began to ban some uses of asbestos, including the spraying of asbestos-containing materials (1973), certain asbestos pipe coverings (1975), artificial fireplace logs made of asbestos (1977), asbestos-containing hairdryers (1979) and so on.

The amount of asbestos used in the United States has declined. In 1973, 880,000 tons were used. By 1987 usage had fallen to 93,340 tons.

Asbestos removal is a dangerous job. When asbestos ages and is disturbed, it releases microscopic fibers into the air that can be inhaled. Once inside the lungs, they can penetrate and irritate lung cells.

DDT and Its Relatives

Another major group of toxic substances are halogenated hydrocarbons. Hydrocarbons are compounds consisting of hydrogen and carbon. Methane, benzene, ethylene, xylene and toluene are examples of hydrocarbons. Scientists have developed ways to add atoms of halogens—chlorine, bromine and iodine—to the hydrocarbons, thereby creating new chemicals. For example, by tacking chlorine onto hydrocarbons, chlorohydrocarbons are created. Among these are polychlorinated biphenyls (PCBs). They are made by combining chlorine and hydrocarbons known as phenols.

Halogenated hydrocarbons have a wide range of uses. PCBs are used as insulators in transformers and other electrical machinery. Chlorinated hydrocarbons are used in such pesticides as DDT, dieldrin, chlordane and endrin. Trichloroethylene and perchloroethylene are used as industrial solvents or degreasing agents. Pentachlorophenol (penta) is a wood preservative used to resist termites. Plastics such as vinyl chloride and polyvinyl chloride are made from chlorinated hydrocarbons.

Many halogenated hydrocarbons are carcinogenic. Some cause anemia, skin damage or interfere with reproduction. They tend to accumulate in the environment and in living organisms, therefore presenting long-term dangers.

Dioxins

These chlorohydrocarbons are among the deadliest of all chemicals. They consist of benzene, oxygen and chlorine. The most dangerous of all is 2,3,7,8-tetrachlorodibenzo-p-dioxin (TCDD). It led to the abandonment of Times Beach, Missouri, a once bustling community of 2,000 people southwest of St. Louis. During the early 1970s, waste oil from a chemical manufacturing plant was sprayed on the town's roads to keep down dust. High levels of TCDD were in the oil. A decade later, after reports of illnesses among residents and the deaths of many animals, the levels of dioxin were measured. The levels were so high that residents were told to immediately leave the town. Times Beach became a ghost

town, surrounded by high fences with warning signs that read: "Hazardous Area—Dioxin—Keep Out."

Dioxins have been found at many sites where wastes from chemical manufacturers are buried, stored or handled. The sediments of the Great Lakes and large river systems, especially near urban areas, contain dioxins. Dioxins can be broken down by sunlight. But they can persist for years in soil. Some types have been shown to have lasted in the ground for more than 15 years.

Dioxins also persist in people and animals, where they accumulate in tissues. Trace levels have been found in the blood, breast milk and fatty tissues of humans and animals from many countries. Plants also accumulate the chemicals. In 1988, the EPA reported that when root crops such as carrots, potatoes and onions are grown in contaminated soils, they can develop dioxin levels that equal or exceed those in the soil itself.

Laboratory studies show that dioxins are extremely poisonous to animals. A single dose of 6 millionths of a gram of TCDD will kill a rat. Nonlethal doses can cause cancer, liver

Various chemicals are used to control crop-damaging insects or environmental annoyances such as high levels of dust on town roads. These chemicals are most often applied by cropdusters from the air, but their effects on the environment and the creatures that inhabit it is still widely disputed.

damage, hair loss and birth defects in laboratory animals. It also damages their immune systems, making them more vulnerable to bacterial and viral diseases.

The effects on people are less certain. Exposure to high levels during industrial accidents causes various short-term problems, including a severe kind of acne called chloracne. Exposure to low levels over long periods of time may cause cancer or other problems, but this has not been proven. There also is concern that the dioxins in breast milk pose a high risk for breast-fed babies. One study indicated that babies who nurse may be exposed to as much as 200 times more dioxin than most adults.

Dioxins are not manufactured deliberately, except in small amounts for research purposes. Most are by-products created during the manufacture of chemicals called chlorophenols, and the products made from them. These products include wood preservatives and disinfectants. Dioxins may also form in incinerators when various organic compounds are burned at low temperatures.

Another source of dioxins are pulp and paper mills that use a chlorine bleaching process during the manufacture of certain types of paper. Some of the dioxins that form during the process end up in the paper. Some are emitted into the atmosphere. And some end up in water wastes, contaminating water downstream from the mills.

Milk cartons, coffee filters, paper towels and plates, TV-dinner containers, disposable diapers—almost any consumer product made from pulp may contain traces of dioxins. The dioxins can contaminate foods and get on people's hands during handling of the products. When the items are discarded, the dioxins may be released into the air, either from the landfill or in ashes emitted by the incinerator. Once in the atmosphere, they can be inhaled by people. They can also contaminate food crops.

Household Poisons

The average American home contains an almost unending list of hazardous chemicals. They can be hazardous to the people using them. And they are hazardous to the environment when they are discarded. For instance, many all-purpose cleaners contain ammonia. Others contain chlorine. Each is harmful to human health: ammonia damages lung tissue and chlorine can form cancer-causing compounds. An even worse problem develops when cleaners containing the two chemicals are mixed. Then deadly chloramine gas is formed.

Mothballs are made from paradichlorobenzene, which can cause liver and kidney damage. Plastic shower curtains give off polyvinyl chloride gas. Air fresheners and permanent-ink markers emit hydrocarbons such as xylene and toluene. Paint, paint thinners, paint removers, wood preservatives, adhesives, oven cleaners, drain openers, wood and metal cleaners, grease and rust solvents, starter fluids, herbicides, pesticides, automotive oil, antifreeze, fuel additives, carburetor cleaners—the list of toxic products found in homes goes on and on.

According to data collected by Dana Duxbury and Associates of Andover, Massachusetts, the average American home generates 15 pounds (6.8 kilograms) of hazardous waste a year. Duxbury says, "most of it goes into local landfills, sewage-treatment plants and septic tanks—all ill-equipped to handle toxins safely."

What are the alternatives? In a few situations, there are none. But with a little effort—and sometimes with no effort at all—people can avoid polluting the environment with these toxins. For example, most service stations have environmentally acceptable methods of disposing of motor oil, antifreeze and other automotive fluids. People who do their own car maintenance can take these liquids to the stations and ask that they be added to the stations' storage drums.

Some communities have facilities where residents can drop off hazardous wastes. Others have or are developing hazardous waste disposal programs.

In many cases, the best alternative is not to use the products in the first place. Many toxic products marketed for home use can be replaced by nontoxic alternatives. (See Chapter 9.)

HAZARDOUS WASTE DISPOSAL

The risks of hazardous wastes are now apparent to many people. As a result, people have put increasing pressure on government agencies and industries to develop safe disposal methods for the substances. Many nations have strict laws addressing the issue. Enforcement of the laws may be weak, however, because the responsible agencies lack the money and personnel to do the job. As a result of this and other factors, the practice of improperly disposing of hazardous materials continues. On the other hand, many companies and individuals are taking whatever steps are needed to comply with disposal regulations or even to go beyond these regulations.

Disposal Choices

One industrial practice that is gaining favor is treating hazardous wastes to neutralize them or make them less toxic. For example, the acidic wastes produced by metal finishing factories can be neutralized by adding alkalines. Precipitators can be used to remove metal from the wastewaters of iron and steel mills.

Another technique uses single-celled organisms called bacteria to break down wastes into safe substances. The process is called bioremediation. For example, bacteria of the genus *Flavobacterium* feed on the toxic wood preservative

Opposite page:
Safe disposal techniques for hazardous waste require strict adherence to procedure. Irresponsible disposal practices or poorly supervised disposal sights can seriously endanger the health and well-being of entire communities.

penta. They break penta down to carbon dioxide, water and harmless chlorides.

The concept of bioremediation is not new. Bacteria have been used for almost a century to process municipal sewage. (See Chapter 8.) Food processors have used microorganisms for more than 20 years to reduce the amount of organic wastes they dump into sewers or waterways. Most organic chemistry factories also use bioremediation.

Secure Landfills

Modern landfills are designed to isolate hazardous wastes from the rest of the environment. They have two liners. These liners are separated by a seepage collection system that collects any leaks from the inner liner. This system is monitored to detect any leakage. Another monitoring system outside the liners detects leakage into the soil and underlying groundwater.

Many experts consider the landfills to be only temporary solutions. They believe that the liners will eventually develop cracks. If this happens, the wastes will have to be removed from the landfill. Otherwise, contamination of the environment will occur.

In some cases, wastes are solidified before being placed in landfills. Cement or other substances are mixed with the toxic wastes to solidify them. This enables the wastes to be more safely and permanently buried.

Deep Well Injection

In this procedure, liquid wastes are pumped or drained into sandstone or limestone hundreds of feet below the Earth's surface. The rock formations are very porous and have the ability to hold massive quantities of liquids.

Deep well injection has been used by steel, chemical, pharmaceutical and other factories for on-site disposal of their hazardous wastes. Proponents say that the rock formations are isolated from groundwater supplies. Opponents aren't convinced this is true. They point out that any leakage of the wastes into groundwater could cause serious, irreversible damage.

Injecting liquids into deep rock formations affects pressure. There is concern that this may create problems. In the 1960s, more than 175 million gallons (660 million liters) of wastes were emptied into a deep well at the U.S. Army's Rocky Mountain Arsenal in Denver, Colorado. This practice is believed by many to have been the cause of Denver's first earthquake in 80 years. Over the following years, there were some 1,500 quakes and tremors of varying intensities. When the army stopped deep well injection of its wastes, the earthquakes stopped, too.

Also in the 1960s, some 150,000 gallons (568,000 liters) of wastes a day were being pumped into a well in Erie, Pennsylvania. The underground pressure became so great that one day a giant geyser shot high into the air. It took workers three weeks to cap the well. During those three weeks, some 4 million gallons (15 million liters) of wastes gushed out onto the land's surface.

Incineration

Burning hazardous wastes other than heavy metals and certain noncombustibles at very high temperatures—over 2,400°F (1,300°C)—greatly reduces their volume. At these temperatures, organic compounds such as PCBs and dioxin are completely destroyed. Experts stress the importance of

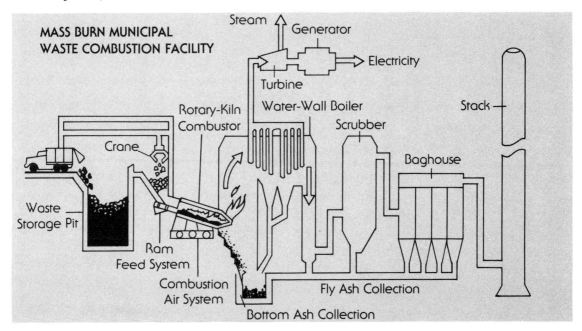

MASS BURN MUNICIPAL WASTE COMBUSTION FACILITY

TOXIC LOVE

In early 1978, Love Canal was a bustling suburb of Niagara Falls, New York. By the end of the year, many of its houses were abandoned and boarded up. The grass, once neatly trimmed, was tall and filled with weeds. The field where children once played was deserted. But on that field, the cause of the mass exodus was easily seen: a poisonous black ooze bubbled up from the ground.

Love Canal had its start in the 1890s, when an entrepreneur named William Love hoped to build a community where factories, power plants and workers' homes could be in close proximity. He began digging a canal to divert water from the Niagara River but had to abandon the venture when the 1903 depression led to his bankruptcy.

In the 1920s, the city and local chemical manufacturers began using the canal as a dump site for municipal and industrial wastes. In 1947, the land was acquired by the Hooker Chemical and Plastics Corporation. During the next several years, Hooker dumped hundreds of large waste-filled drums into the canal. Then in 1953 it covered the canal with dirt and sold the land to Niagara Falls for a token $1. The city built an elementary school and play-

ground. It divided the rest of the land into residential building lots. Most of the people who bought the lots and built on them did not know Love Canal's poisonous history.

By the early 1970s, however, black ooze and smelly fluids were leaking into basements, surfacing in backyards and forming pools in the school playground. Trees turned black and died suddenly. Sections of ground sank. Potholes formed and were filled with reddish gunk. Children playing outdoors returned home with skin rashes and rotting sneakers. People began experiencing an abnormally large number of health problems; rates of mental retardation, miscarriages, birth defects, epilepsy, nervous disorders, liver diseases and rectal bleeding were all above normal.

In 1978, in response to residents' complaints, state and federal agencies investigated. They found 82 chemicals in the ground, air and water. Among these chemicals were 11 known carcinogens and 6 known mutagens. President Jimmy Carter declared Love Canal a national emergency area. Residents were advised to move immediately, and the state began buying up people's homes. Some people stayed. But about 700 families abandoned their homes, leaving

their contaminated belongings.

Eventually, about 200 homes closest to the dump were demolished. The toxic wastes in the canal were encased in layers of clay and plastic. Then the area was covered with soil and grass, and fenced off.

Following tests during the late 1980s, the state and federal government decided that much of the Love Canal area was safe enough to permit people to move back in. They said that living in the area would pose no greater risk than living in other areas of Niagara Falls.

"It has all the characteristics of a terrific neighborhood," said James E. Carr, director of planning for the Love Canal Area Revitalization Agency, which was selling the houses at about 20% less than the cost of comparable houses in nearby suburbs. "The first people in will certainly be getting themselves a bargain, because they're pioneers of a sort."

Many environmentalists were appalled by the decision. They tried to prevent the sales. One activist, reminding people that there are more than 200 toxic dump sites in the Niagara Falls area, commented that comparing Love Canal with other contaminated neighborhoods "is like comparing rotten oranges with rotten oranges."

the high temperatures; at lower incineration temperatures, hazardous wastes may contaminate fly ash and be released into the atmosphere.

A highly controversial practice that is banned in most places is ocean incineration. It involves burning hazardous wastes in incinerators mounted on ocean-going vessels. Supporters say that the practice avoids exposing people to possible toxic releases. They also contend that toxic hydrogen chloride gas produced during incineration is neutralized by seawater. Opponents question this. They say the companies are simply avoiding the need for expensive scrubbing equipment. They point out that the companies also avoid liability if an accident occurs, because any damage to the ocean waters or to marine life would be difficult to trace. The companies couldn't get away with this on land, claim environmentalists. But, as they point out, "fish don't vote."

Cleaning Up Waste Sites

Throughout the world, thousands of sites have been used for the disposal of hazardous wastes. The total number in the United States is unknown. By 1990, however, the U.S. Environmental Protection Agency had listed 1,207 sites in the United States on its National Priorities List. These are the sites that potentially pose the greatest threats to the nation's public health and environment. New Jersey led the list, with 109 sites. Other states high on the list were Pennsylvania (95), California (88), New York (83) and Michigan (78).

No one knows how much it will cost to clean up contaminated sites. But everyone agrees it will be very, very expensive. The Office of Technology Assessment, a research branch of the U.S. Congress, has estimated that costs in the United States alone could reach $100 billion.

Generally, cleanup operations involve digging up waste containers and contaminated soil, then transporting these to approved hazardous waste incinerators or landfills. Contaminated water can be partially cleansed of some contaminants. For example, dissolved organic compounds can be removed by using a carbon filtering process.

FROM CRADLE TO GRAVE

The garbage hauler picked up a load of toxic wastes from the hospital. Hospital administrators paid the hauler to cart the wastes to an approved landfill. But the wastes never arrived. The hauler had pocketed the money—and dumped the wastes down a mountainside.

To help prevent such scams, legislatures are passing laws that require "cradle-to-grave" monitoring of infectious and hazardous wastes. This monitoring is designed to prove that the wastes actually reached an approved destination.

Under this system, garbage haulers must have a special permit to cart hazardous wastes. On a manifest—a printed list of their cargo—they must indicate where the wastes were picked up and what type of wastes are being transported. They have to identify the facility where the wastes are being taken and present evidence that the facility has agreed to accept the wastes. Finally, a record of receipt of the wastes must be provided by the facility.

A BAKE-OUT IS NOT A COOK-OUT

A large group of substances called volatile organic compounds become gases at room temperature. They include such toxic chemicals as benzene, carbon tetrachloride, formaldehyde and styrene. These can be found in some paint, furniture, upholstery, carpeting, draperies and construction materials—as well as many other products.

In an office building with insufficient ventilation, the effects may be so severe that many people working in the building complain of headaches, eye or throat irritation, itchy skin, nausea, fatigue or difficulty in concentrating. The problem even has a name: sick-building syndrome.

Any building may occasionally experience indoor air-quality problems. But sick-building syndrome appears to be most common in new and renovated buildings. A World Health Organization Committee estimated that up to 30% of new and remodeled buildings may have such problems.

Some buildings have reduced the problem by improving ventilation. Another method that is being tested is the bake-out. For a few days, the temperature in an empty new building is raised to close to 100°F (38°C). In theory, the high temperature speeds the evaporation of the volatile organic compounds.

A look at five California buildings that were "baked" showed a wide discrepancy in success rates. The concentration of volatile organic compounds fell from 0% in one building to a high of 95% in another.

Bioremediation

Bioremediation is also being used with some success to clean up toxic waste sites and polluted water. At the present time, it is effective for only certain chemical wastes, and only in certain situations. But scientists are working to expand the uses of this clean-up approach. Much of the interest in this procedure stems from the fact that it promises to be cheaper, safer and more effective than landfills or incineration. Also, it may be useful for dealing with contaminated land under buildings.

Some scientists are trying to create special bacteria in laboratories. Most interest, however, has focused on microorganisms that occur naturally in the environment. Many types of bacteria exist in hazardous waste sites. Normally, however, their populations are too small to handle all the wastes. Scientists collect the bacteria and try to find ways to make them reproduce more rapidly. Usually, this requires getting more oxygen and nutrients into their environment. One way to do this at a dump site is to pump in air to raise the oxygen content and add fertilizers that contain nitrogen and other essential elements. When the bacteria have finished eating all the wastes, the populations die off, returning to prepollution levels.

Each type of bacterium may attack only one type of chemical. Thus dump sites containing a variety of chemicals may need to be treated with many different kinds of bacteria. Among the biggest challenges to scientists are PCBs. There are more than 200 varieties of PCBs, and all PCB products contain mixtures of different varieties. In a typical dump site, there may be more than 100 types of PCBs—and the mixture in one dump site may be very different from the mixture in another dump site.

In some cases, the environment is too cold or otherwise unsuitable for rapid bacterial growth. Then the contaminated soil or water can be removed and placed—together with the appropriate bacteria—in a closed chamber called a bioreactor. Temperatures, nutrient levels and other factors within the bioreactor can be regulated to create an ideal environment for the bacteria.

Three bioreactors, each able to hold 60 cubic yards (46 cubic meters) of soil, were used to help clean up pesticide contamination in Minot, North Dakota, in 1987. In two weeks, bacteria had reduced the levels of the two most plentiful pesticides from 800 parts per million to 10 parts per million in 750 cubic yards (573 cubic meters) of treated soil.

6

RADIOACTIVE WASTES

On December 2, 1942, history was made at the University of Chicago. The world's first successful nuclear reactor began operating. Within the reactor's core, uranium atoms were split, in a self-sustaining chain reaction, to release large amounts of energy.

Other reactors soon built at Oak Ridge, Tennessee, and at Hanford, Washington, produced material for nuclear bombs. Then, soon after World War II ended in 1945, nations began to develop and promote peaceful uses of nuclear power.

By the 1950s, this new source of energy was called the energy of the future. Proponents said it was safe, cheap, easy to produce and almost inexhaustible. In 1956, a reactor at Cumberland, England, began producing commercial power. In 1957, the first U.S. commercial nuclear power plant began operating at Shippingport, Pennsylvania.

Today, more than 400 commercial nuclear power plants are in operation worldwide. France is the world's leading user of nuclear energy: about 65% of its electricity is produced in nuclear power plants. Other leaders include Belgium (60%), Sweden (50%), Switzerland (40%), Finland (38%), West Germany (30%) and Japan (22%). In the United States, there are over 100 such plants. They produce about 18% of the electricity consumed in the nation.

The industry's growth has not matched the hopes expressed by its supporters back in the 1950s, however. Many

Opposite page: Radioactive wastes remain dangerous for the longest amount of time. Three Mile Island in Pennsylvania, shown here, is one of more than 400 nuclear power plants currently in operation worldwide that produce radioactive wastes.

51

ELEMENTS, ATOMS AND ISOTOPES

The basic component of all matter is the atom. It is the smallest part of an element that has all the chemical properties of that element. Break apart an oxygen atom, and it no longer is oxygen. Split a uranium atom, and it no longer is uranium.

Atoms are incredibly tiny, but they are made up of even smaller particles called protons, neutrons and electrons. Protons have a positive electrical charge. Neutrons have no electrical charge; they are neutral. Electrons have a negative electrical charge. The protons and neutrons are in the center, or nucleus, of the atom. The electrons orbit the nucleus.

All atoms that have the same number of protons in their nuclei belong to the same element. All atoms with eight protons are oxygen atoms. All atoms with 92 protons are uranium atoms.

Most atoms have an equal number of protons and electrons.

But the number of neutrons may vary. For example, an atom of ordinary hydrogen consists of one proton and one electron. It does not contain any neutrons. But there are two other kinds of hydrogen. One kind, deuterium, has one proton, one electron and one neutron. Another kind, tritium, has one proton, one electron and two neutrons.

Atoms of an element with different numbers of neutrons are called isotopes. Elements with large atoms, such as uranium, have many isotopes. The most common isotope of uranium has 92 protons and 146 neutrons in its nucleus. It is called uranium-238, or U-238 for short (92+146=238). Another isotope is U-235, which has 92 protons and 143 neutrons in its nucleus. In addition, there are rarer isotopes, running the gamut from U-227 to U-240.

The particles in the nucleus are held together by a force called "binding energy." In large atoms, the nucleus does not have enough binding energy to hold it together. It is unstable, or radioactive. It breaks down, giving off some of its contents as radiation in the form of particles and high-energy rays.

If an atom gives off one or more of its neutrons, it becomes another isotope of the same element. But if it gives off one or more of its protons, it is no longer the same element. It has decayed into another element. In nature, uranium-235 naturally decays into thorium-231.

Radioactive forms of an element are called radioisotopes. Lead-211, for example, is a radioisotope that decays eventually to form lead-207, which is a stable isotope. Some radioisotopes are products of natural radioactive decay. Many more are created in nuclear reactors.

communities have fought construction of nuclear power plants in their areas. Some countries, such as Denmark, have no nuclear plants. People in these places consider nuclear energy unsafe. The major problem is radiation: harmful particles and rays that are emitted when uranium and other radioactive atoms break down, or decay. This radiation can cause disease or death in humans and other organisms.

The nuclear power and nuclear weapons industries produce large amounts of radioactive materials. Other sources include hospitals, dental offices and research laboratories. There are natural sources, too, including cosmic rays and radioactive substances in soil, rocks and water.

Unstable Atoms and Radiation

The atoms of uranium and some other elements are unstable. They decay into smaller atoms. In the process, radiation is given off. This radiation is in the form of alpha particles, beta particles and gamma rays.

An alpha particle is positively charged and consists of two neutrons and two protons. A beta particle is a negatively charged electron. Gamma radiation is similar to X rays but it has much more energy.

Alpha radiation is the least penetrating kind of radiation. It can be stopped by human skin, thin clothing or a sheet of paper. It can, however, enter a person's body during breathing or along with food or water. Then it can damage lung or digestive system tissues. The tailings (waste materials) produced during uranium mining emit significant amounts of alpha radiation. Plutonium, produced in nuclear reactors, also is an alpha emitter.

Beta radiation is more penetrating than alpha radiation. It can pass through skin. It can also enter the body during breathing and swallowing. If these substances become concentrated in the body, they can be dangerous. Strontium-90, which has been found in some cow milk, tends to concentrate in people's bones, where it gives off radiation that can damage bone marrow. Beta radiation can be stopped by a thin sheet of aluminum or by a thick piece of wood.

Gamma radiation is very penetrating. It can pass right through the human body, damaging any cells in its path. Iodine-131 emits gamma rays as well as beta particles. This substance can become concentrated in the thyroid gland. To stop gamma radiation, heavy shielding, such as a thick wall of concrete, is needed.

Some radioactive substances occur in nature. Radon and uranium are found in rocks and soil. Radioactive isotopes of many other elements also exist.

Other radioactive substances are produced in nuclear reactors but are seldom found in nature. Called transuranic elements, their atoms are larger than those of uranium. There are 10 transuranic elements, including the very dangerous plutonium.

THE URANIUM-238 DECAY CHAIN

Radioactive Element	Minutes	Half-Life Days	Years
Uranium-238			4.5 billion
Thorium-234		24.1	
Protactinium-234	1.2		
Uranium-234			247,000
Thorium-230			80,000
Radium-226			1,622
Radon-222		3.8	
Polonium-218	3.0		
Lead-214	26.8		
Bismuth-214	19.7		
Polonium-214	0.00016 second		
Lead-210			22
Bismuth-210		5.0	
Polonium-210		138.3	
Lead-206		Stable	

Many Half-Lives

Every radioisotope decays at a specific rate. (See chart "The Uranium-238 Decay Chain" on page 53.) The time needed for an isotope to lose its radioactivity is measured by using its half-life. This is the time needed for half the atoms in a sample of the isotope to decay. The half-life of strontium-90 is 28 years. If you begin with a sample of 10,000 strontium-90 atoms, after 28 years, 5,000 radioactive atoms would remain.

Scientists believe that it takes 10 to 20 half-lives for a radioactive substance to become safe. For strontium-90, this is at least 280 years. For plutonium-239, which has a half-life of 24,000 years, this is almost a quarter of a million years!

The Effects of Radiation

Radiation disrupts the chemical processes that take place in living cells. It damages the cells, decreasing resistance to disease. In humans, it increases the probability of becoming sterile or developing anemia and cancer. For example, if enough strontium-90 is present in the bone marrow, where white blood cells are formed, the radiation given off by the strontium may cause cancer of the white blood cells, a disease called leukemia.

Sometimes, radiation causes mutations, or changes, in genes. These are the structures in cells that pass on characteristics from one generation to the next. Mutations are almost always harmful. If mutations occur in reproductive cells (eggs and sperm), they can cause miscarriages or defects such as Down's syndrome (a type of mental retardation).

Like other hazardous wastes, radioactive substances can move through a food chain. Along the Columbia River, a radioactive form of phosphorous released from the Hanford nuclear weapons plant near Richland, Washington, contaminated bacteria and algae. These were eaten by fish and shellfish, which were later eaten by people.

Radiation doses are measured in rem, which stands for "roentgen equivalent man." One rem equals one thousand millirems. An average American receives about 360 millirems of radiation annually. More than half of this comes from radon gas and other naturally occurring substances. The remainder comes from artificial sources. A chest X-ray, for example, exposes a person to 10 millirems of radiation. A round-trip flight across North America results in an exposure of about 5 millirems.

When an accident occurs at a nuclear plant, a person may be exposed to large amounts of radiation over a period of a few hours. Exposure to 700 rems or more in a short time means certain death. Exposure to 100 to 700 rems causes radiation sickness, some deaths, and an increased risk of cancer.

Exposure to lesser amounts of radiation is believed to be harmful, too, because the effects are cumulative. That is, the more radiation a person is exposed to over a period of time, the greater the possibility of damage. This is difficult to measure, for two reasons. First, the cause-and-effect relationship is not immediate; it may take many years for damage to become apparent. It can be 25 years or longer before cancer develops. Second, over a period of time, other factors—smoking or exposure to toxic chemicals, for example—can confuse the issue.

Evidence is usually obtained by studying the amount of illness in people who have received only low doses of radiation. For example, before the 1970s, wastes produced during uranium mining were believed to emit too little radiation to harm people. As a result, miners did not wear protective clothing. Today, very high rates of cancer are occurring among these miners.

Studies have also looked at people who are exposed to low-level radiation and the possible increased risk of cancer to their unborn children. Most studies have indicated that there is no connection. The biggest study, done over a 40-year-period, followed men who survived the atomic bomb attacks on the Japanese cities of Hiroshima and Nagasaki at the end of World War II. Presumably the men were exposed to large doses of radiation during the bomb explosions. Yet no excess cancer cases have been seen in children conceived by the men following the war.

In 1990, however, a study reported by epidemiologist Martin J. Gardner of the British Medical Research Council,

DANGER: RADON

You cannot see it, smell it or taste it. But it is found almost everywhere—and it can be dangerous. It is called radon.

Radon is a radioactive gas formed during the decay of uranium. It is found in rocks and soils that naturally contain uranium. It is also found in certain kinds of industrial wastes, such as the by-products from uranium and phosphate mining.

In outdoor air, radon is diluted and dispersed to very low levels. But when radon becomes trapped in an enclosed space, such as a home, it can accumulate and become a health hazard. It can increase people's risk of developing lung cancer. In the United States, an estimated 5,000 to 20,000 lung cancer deaths each year may be caused by exposure to radon.

Radon enters buildings through dirt floors, cracks in concrete floors and basement walls, floor drains and other openings. It may also enter through well water.

Measuring instruments called radon detectors can be used to determine the level of radon in a building. In some places, these are available from local governments. Typically, however, people must purchase testing kits or hire trained personnel to conduct the tests.

In many cases, increasing ventilation and sealing cracks will adequately lower radon levels in the air. Radon-contaminated well water can be treated by aeration or filtration through granular activated carbon.

indicated there may be a danger. In Seascale, England, there is a nuclear reprocessing plant called Sellafield (formerly Windscale). Children born less than 3 miles (5 kilometers) from Sellafield suffer leukemia, a cancer of the white blood cells, at a rate five times the national average. Similar clusters of leukemia cases have been found near other nuclear facilities in England and Scotland.

Gardner concluded that the best explanation was having a father who worked at Sellafield. Almost all the sick children's fathers worked there. Moreover, the fathers had received high doses of radiation—though well within limits considered safe—shortly before the children were conceived. Gardner suspected that the radiation caused a mutation in the fathers' sperm cells. When passed on to children, the mutation increased their risk of leukemia.

Does this contradict the studies in Japan? Not necessarily. Scientists pointed out that very few children were conceived in Japan right after the bombings.

In 1990, the International Commission on Radiological Protection recommended that the maximum allowable radiation dose for workers be cut to 2 rem per year. Previously the level had been set at 5 rem per year. The step was taken, said commission chairman Dr. Dan J. Beninson, because workers receiving exposures close to 5 rem per year for many years, "have run a higher level of risk than we expected."

Kinds of Waste

There are five major kinds of radioactive wastes. They differ in how they are produced, their level of radioactivity and their potential hazard.

Tailings

During the mining and processing of uranium, large quantities of sandy wastes called tailings are produced. These contain radioactive isotopes of thorium, radium and radon, all of which emit low levels of radiation.

The uranium ore is converted to uranium dioxide that is formed into pellets about the size of pencil erasers. The pellets are loaded into metal cases to make long cylindrical fuel rods. During the manufacturing processes, some low-level radioactive gases enter the atmosphere. Low-level liquid and solid radioactive wastes are also produced.

Spent Fuel

Bundles of fuel rods are installed in the core of the nuclear reactor. Once the reactor is started, high-energy neutrons speed through the fuel rods, striking uranium nuclei. The nuclei split into smaller nuclei and emit further neutrons; this is fission. These neutrons strike other uranium nuclei, and the fission process is repeated. This chain reaction will continue as long as enough uranium nuclei are available. Theoretically, a nuclear reactor can operate for years without replacing the fuel rods. However, the reactor operates more efficiently if about one-third of the fuel rods are replaced each year.

The rods that are removed from a reactor are called spent fuel. They are still highly radioactive and they generate a lot of heat. They contain unused uranium, plutonium-239 that was created during the nuclear reaction and waste products such as strontium-90 and cesium-137.

High-Level Wastes

Fuel rods can be reprocessed to extract the unused uranium and the plutonium, so that these can be used again. The remaining wastes are intensely radioactive. They are in liquid form, though they can be treated to form a mixture of liquid and sludge or a dry substance called calcine.

Transuranic Wastes

Plutonium and other transuranic elements form when uranium absorbs extra particles instead of splitting. Small amounts of these elements are produced at commercial nuclear power plants, but the main sources of these wastes are nuclear reprocessing plants. They are not as intensively radioactive as other high-level wastes, but they take much longer to decay. They are the longest living kind of radioactive wastes.

Low-Level Wastes

Low-level wastes include all items that become contaminated as they come in contact with radioactive material. They include protective clothing, tools, machines, filters, research materials such as test tubes, paper towels and cleaning rags. Weapons facilities, nuclear power plants, industrial firms, hospitals and research laboratories produce low-level wastes.

The Disposal Problem

During the first few decades of the so-called Nuclear Age, little attention was given to radioactive wastes. Mine tailings were considered harmless. They were left in huge piles that were easily accessible to playing children and other people. Some were used as landfill and had homes built on them. In Grand Junction, Colorado, tailings were even used in the foundations and walls of homes, schools and churches.

Radioactive gases were frequently vented into the atmosphere. Low-level wastes were dumped into oceans and rivers. Wastes that would be radioactive for thousands of years were stored in tanks designed to last 40 years.

Wastes piled up. There were many instances of radiation leaks. An explosion in a waste-storage tank at the Hanford Site in Washington lifted the tank 6 feet (1.8 meters) off its foundation and produced a 50-foot- (15-meter-) high geyser of radioactive steam. Rain-soaked tailings were carried downriver in New Mexico, polluting the environment with radiation for a distance of 75 miles (121 kilometers). Plutonium was found in the flesh of edible fish at an ocean dump site near California's Farrallon Islands.

Tailings

Huge piles of tailings have been produced during uranium mining. In the United States, most tailings are located in sparsely populated parts of Arizona, New Mexico, Utah and Wyoming. Wind has blown some of the tailings onto land where livestock and wild animals graze.

Ideally, tailings should be buried. But this has generally been considered too costly. The best alternative is to cover tailings with thick layers of soil. Too often, however, they are simply left in huge uncovered piles, exposed to the air and subject to erosion and leaching.

Fuel Rods

The fuel rods removed from a nuclear reactor contain both high-level wastes and transuranic wastes. The spent fuel can be reprocessed to remove and reuse most of the uranium and plutonium that it contains. This is done in France, West Germany and Japan and in most U.S. weapons facilities.

Wastes from U.S. commercial nuclear power plants are not currently being reprocessed. Instead, the spent fuel rods are kept at the bottom of 20 foot (6 meter) tanks of water. The water cools the rods and absorbs neutrons. This system is not designed for long-term use. But more than 16,500 tons of spent fuel are estimated to be stored in pools. Some has been in storage for 30 years or longer. The pools at several power plants are nearing capacity.

High-Level Wastes

When fuel is reprocessed, the remaining wastes are very radioactive. They must be completely isolated from the environment. Because of uncertainty over how to handle the wastes, they have generally been stored, untreated, in temporary containers, sometimes for decades. At the Hanford Site, 64 million gallons (242 million liters) of highly radioactive wastes have been stored in giant tanks for as long as 40 years.

In France and some other countries, high-level wastes are fused in molten glass, which is then solidified and embedded in concrete or stainless-steel containers. The process is called vitrification. The glass and the containers are not expected to disintegrate for many centuries, by which time the level of radioactivity will have fallen to a level comparable to that of uranium ore. At the present time, the vitrified wastes produced in France are stored in underground vaults. Eventually, the government plans to bury them.

ALASKA

HAWAII

ATOMIC RESIDUE

The United States is littered with contaminated processing plants, laboratories, nuclear reactors and testing grounds left by the atomic weapons industry.

Transuranic Wastes

Before 1970, transuranic wastes were generally dumped in unlined trenches with low-level wastes. This led to contamination of soil and water supplies. Cleaning up such sites is difficult, time-consuming and very expensive.

Today, transuranic wastes are stored in special stainless steel containers, awaiting permanent disposal.

Low-Level Wastes

Initially, low-level wastes were buried in unlined trenches or placed in steel drums and dumped at sea. Dangerous wastes, including transuranic elements, were often mixed in with the low-level wastes, either legally or illegally.

Today, low-level wastes are placed in containers that will not leak for at least 100 years. These are buried in specially constructed landfills lined with clay and plastic sheeting, both of which theoretically prevent leakage. Clay coverings are put over the landfills to prevent the escape of radioactive gases. Even with these precautions, however, it is possible that water will infiltrate the landfill, pick up radioactive materials, then seep to the outside environment.

Many of these landfills in the United States are quickly becoming full. Efforts to build new disposal sites face a great deal of opposition from people living nearby.

In some places, radioactive materials that decay in a few months have been disposed of in municipal landfills and incinerators. Certain consumer products that contain radioactive materials, such as smoke detectors and glow-in-the-dark watches, also are allowed in municipal landfills and incinerators. In 1990, the U.S. Nuclear Regulatory Commission set a new policy. It would allow nuclear facilities to dispose of work gloves and other mildly radioactive materials in municipal landfills or incinerators as long as any single disposal does not expose any person to an annual dose of more than 10 millirems. "If we are able to establish a list of things that we don't need to worry about as regulators, this would obviously give us more time to worry about—and deal with—real problems," said Kenneth M. Carr, chairman of the commission. Environmentalists, consumer advocates and the EPA all called the new policy too lenient.

Permanent Disposal Facilities

Nations are trying to find a safe, permanent disposal method for high-level wastes, transuranic wastes and spent fuel. To ensure safety, these wastes must be isolated from the environment for many generations. Exactly how long a time is needed is debated. Some people believe that an isolation time of 300 to 500 years is sufficient. This figure is based on the half-lives of abundant radioisotopes such as strontium-90 and cesium-137. Others say that isolation times should be based on long-lived radioisotopes such as plutonium, although these are present in much smaller quantities.

Various disposal ideas have been proposed. In the 1970s, the idea of rocketing the wastes into space was considered. One proposal was to use space shuttles to carry the wastes into orbits around the Earth. Then a second vehicle could be used to propel the wastes into an orbit around the sun. Another proposal was to fire the wastes into the sun. Still another was to isolate the wastes on the moon, permitting future recovery if technology develops a use for them. Both the high cost and the danger of an accident during launch, resulting in catastrophic releases of radioactive wastes into the atmosphere, made these ideas infeasible.

Investigators from several countries are studying the possibility of isolating nuclear wastes in sediments beneath the oceans. In the middle of the north Pacific and north Atlantic oceans there are thick, stable sediments that have been accumulating for millions of years. It might be possible to place nuclear wastes within these sediments. One concern is the possible effect on the sediments of the heat generated by the wastes. Also, like space disposal, such a plan would require international agreement.

At the present time, the preferred plan is to store the wastes at least 1,000 feet (300 meters) underground, in a repository carved out of rock. This would be done in a geologically stable area, where earthquakes and volcanoes would not be a problem and where there was little possibility that groundwater might leach wastes and carry them toward aquifers or toward the surface. Barriers—some natural, others human-made—would isolate the wastes.

In the United States, an act passed by Congress in 1982 required the Department of Energy to build an underground repository for wastes from commercial nuclear power plants. The repository was to be ready by 1998. This deadline will not be met. Finding a suitable site has been difficult. One site nominated by the department is on the Ogallala aquifer in Texas. If there were leakage from the repository, the aquifer—the nation's largest source of groundwater—could be poisoned.

In 1988, Yucca Mountain, Nevada, was nominated as the site for the nation's first underground repository. The nomination quickly ran into trouble. There was strong opposition to the plan by people who lived nearby. They were skeptical that the wastes could be safely contained for the very long time needed to avoid harm. Environmentalists pointed out that the site is only 12 miles (20 kilometers) from Lathrop Wells, a volcano that may have formed less than 20,000 years ago. The possibility of earthquake activity seems high, particularly after the Department of Energy's data indicated that there are 32 active faults on the site itself.

When and if a permanent repository is built, wastes will have to be transported by truck or train from their current storage places. The wastes will be transported in containers designed to withstand severe accidents. Nonetheless, there is the risk that radiation could be released into the atmosphere.

Closing a Nuclear Plant

During its operation, a nuclear reactor becomes contaminated with radioactivity. The massive concrete shield around the reactor becomes contaminated. So, too, do pipes, drains and other parts of the facility. Plant decommissioning is waste management on a huge scale.

A nuclear reactor is believed to have a useful lifespan of 30 to 40 years. Then it must be shut down, or what is called decommissioned. The site must be cleaned up, to prevent contamination from spreading throughout the environment. Currently, there are three options.

In one method, favored by U.S. utilities, the facility is dismantled immediately following shutdown. Every contaminated item is packaged and shipped to a waste-disposal facility. An alternative method, favored in Canada and France, is to leave the decommissioned plant alone for 50 to 100 years. This would allow a certain amount of radioactive decay to occur before dismantling. In the third method, liquid wastes, fuel and surface contamination is removed to the greatest degree possible. Then the facility is entombed; it is covered with enough concrete or steel to prevent the escape of any remaining radiation.

All methods are technically complex, potentially hazardous and very costly. Decommissioning the United States' first commercial nuclear power plant at Shippingport, Pennsylvania, was completed in 1990. The cost was more than $90 million. The spent reactor vessel was transported 8,100 miles (13,000 kilometers) down the Ohio and Mississippi rivers, into the Gulf of Mexico, through the Panama Canal, up the Pacific coast and up the Columbia River to a burial spot on the Hanford Reservation.

In Missouri, the Weldon Spring plant that processes uranium ore covers 59 acres (24 hectares). In addition to the processing plant, there are four large waste pits and a quarry that was once used to dispose of wastes. In 1988, the U.S. Department of Energy estimated that decommissioning and decontaminating the processing plant would cost $100 million. Cleaning up the waste pits and quarry would cost an additional $437 million.

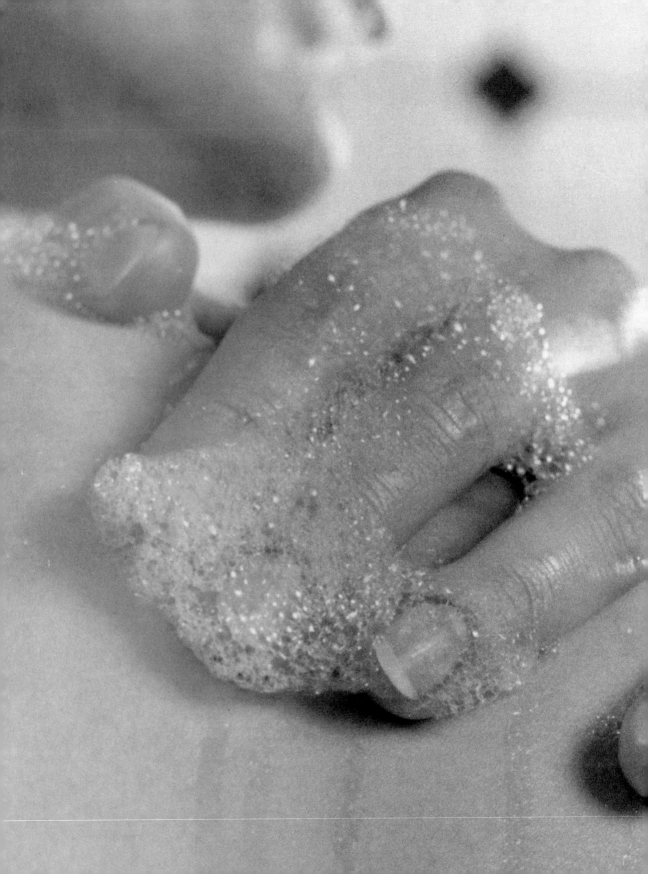

7
WASTEWATERS

Water is your body's most essential nutrient. Every cell in your body depends on water to function properly. In fact, the cells are made up largely of water. Blood is 83% water. Muscles are 75% water. Even bone is 22% water.

To remain healthy, you need to take in more than 2 quarts (1.9 liters) of water every day. This replaces water lost through excretion and perspiration. If you are like most people, you obtain about half of your daily water from liquids: water, milk, fruit juices and so on. The remainder comes from the foods you eat. Foods contain surprisingly large amounts of water. Iceberg lettuce is 96% water, cantaloupe 91%, raw carrots 88%, baked potatoes 75%, ice cream 63% and pizza 48%.

The water you drink and the water in the foods you eat come from surface water and groundwater. If these waters are polluted, then your health can be endangered. The health of plants and animals can also be seriously put at risk.

Unfortunately, almost all of the world's waters are polluted with wastes produced by human beings and our various activities. Some of these wastes are disposed of in the ground as solids or in the air as gases. Others, the subject of this chapter, are disposed of in various kinds of water supplies.

Opposite page:
Every time a person takes a shower, flushes a toilet or washes dishes wastewater and raw sewage are produced.

Sources of Wastewaters

Every time you take a shower, flush a toilet or use a dishwasher you produce raw sewage. Raw sewage is everything that is flushed from bathtubs, toilets, sinks, dishwashers and washing machines. It contains soaps and detergents, urine and feces, toilet paper, strands of hair, kitchen wastes and other contaminants. It all adds up to enormous amounts. An estimated 4.8 billion gallons (18.2 billion liters) of water are flushed from American toilets—each day! Multiply this amount by three and you have the total amount of sewage that originates in American homes daily.

Another form of sewage is the rainwater and melting snow that run off streets into streams and sewers. This wastewater carries solid particles, leaves and other litter. When people wash cars, lawn furniture and other items outdoors, more wastewater is produced.

Industry also produces huge quantities of wastewaters. In 1989, the U.S. Environmental Protection Agency reported that manufacturers in the United States released 9.7 billion pounds (4.4 billion kilograms) of toxic chemicals into streams and other surface waters during 1987. In reality, however, the amount was much higher. Only manufacturers that used more than 10,000 pounds (4,500 kilograms) or produced more than 75,000 pounds (34,000 kilograms) of the chemicals were required to inform the EPA. Moreover, about 25% of the manufacturers who were required to report did not do so. Also, the manufacturers had to report releases of only 300 chemicals. Many other toxic chemicals released into the environment went unreported.

Farming is also a waste source. Silt, fertilizers, pesticides and manure frequently contaminate water. Another source of problems is overapplication of irrigation water. The excess, or waste, water washes into waterways, carrying fertilizers, salts and other chemicals.

Characteristics

The effect of wastewaters on a habitat depends on the composition and volume of the waters. Waters carrying

FISH IN HOT WATER

Billions of gallons of industrial wastewaters are polluted not by chemicals or viruses but by heat—a problem called thermal pollution. Power plants, steel mills, petroleum refineries and other industries use great quantities of cold water to cool equipment. The water is drawn from rivers or other waterways. If it is returned directly to the waterway, it may kill fish or interfere with their reproduction. For example, when the release of hot water caused water temperatures in the Columbia River to rise 5.4°F (3°C), many chinook salmon eggs were killed.

Thermal pollution can be reduced by building cooling tow-

ers. After the water has been used in the power plant or factory, it is circulated through a network of pipes in the towers.

Heat is transferred through the pipes into the atmosphere. Once the water has lost this excess heat, it can then be returned to the waterway.

Another way to reduce thermal pollution is to pump the hot water into a specially built pond near the factory. The water is held in the pond until it cools.

In some cases, thermal pollution is used in a beneficial manner. Some holding ponds are used for recreation. In others, fish like carp, which respond well to warmth, are raised. Carp can live in water as warm as 95°F (35°C). In contrast, lake trout die if the water temperature rises above 75°F (24°C).

heavy concentrations of household wastes are very different from those consisting mostly of rainwater or those discharged by a petroleum refinery. These differences can affect the types of treatment needed to clean the waters.

One important characteristic is the biochemical oxygen demand (BOD). This is the amount of dissolved oxygen needed by microorganisms to decompose organic matter in the water. The greater the amount of organic matter, the higher the BOD.

The kind of organisms present in wastewater is important because some may cause disease. Household wastes generally contain large populations of microorganisms that live in human intestines. For example, it is estimated that the feces eliminated in one day by one person contain one million coliform bacteria! These particular bacteria are not necessarily harmful. But where they exist, harmful species, including hard to detect viruses, can also exist.

Suspended solids are another common group of impurities in water. These include both organic and inorganic particles.

WHAT DO THEY MEAN?

Many terms used by people do not have common, agreed-upon definitions. This can lead to confusion and misunderstandings. Such is sometimes the case with the term *waste reduction*.

Waste reduction does not mean waste treatment. It does not mean concentrating the hazardous content of a waste to reduce waste volume. It does not mean diluting wastes to reduce the degree of hazard. It means avoiding or reducing the *production* of wastes. As a result, the need to treat wastes or discard them is avoided or reduced.

Nor does waste reduction mean controlling one kind of pollution only to produce another kind of pollution. Using air-pollution control devices to prevent toxic wastes from entering the atmosphere sounds great—until you stop to ask what happens to the wastes. Chances are, they are removed from the control devices and dumped in a landfill, where instead of polluting the air they can leach into and pollute groundwater.

To limit confusion and misunderstandings, the term *source reduction* is preferred by many people. It stresses that the subject is avoiding or reducing wastes at the source—not afterward. If wastes are not produced in the first place, they do not have to be dealt with by the producer, consumer or society as a whole.

Algae, clay and silt are examples. They color the water and make it murky. Suspended bacteria, viruses and protozoans may cause disease. And the greater the amount of suspended solids, the larger the amount of sludge, or residue, that may build up at the bottom of a waterway or in a treatment plant.

Many different chemicals may be dissolved in wastewater. These include nitrates and other nutrients, heavy metals, synthetic organic compounds and dissolved gases. Household and agricultural wastewaters usually contain significant amounts of nutrients. Many industrial discharges contain heavy metals and organic compounds. Each chemical may require specialized treatment to remove it from the wastewater or render it harmless. A metal-finishing factory, for example, may use special filters to remove dissolved metals from wastewaters.

The pH of the water indicates acidity. It is represented on a scale of 0 to 14, with 7 being neutral, 0 most acid and 14 most alkaline. If water is too acidic or alkaline, it will harm aquatic organisms. It also will limit the effectiveness of wastewater treatment.

Chlorine demand is the amount of chlorine that reacts with organic and inorganic pollutants in a water sample. It is the difference between the amount of chlorine applied to the water and the amount left at the end of a specified time. It is affected by the amount of pollutants, the pH and the temperature.

Effects of Pollution

Hundreds of thousands of chemicals produced by human activities have entered the water. Each chemical has a unique effect. Some may be beneficial. Others are harmful even in extremely small amounts.

Many chemicals become increasingly dangerous as they react with one another in water. This is true with bleach, a common household and industrial cleaner that is frequently part of sewage. Bleaches contain sodium or calcium hypochlorite. As these chemicals decompose they give off individual oxygen atoms, which "burn up" many kinds of organic matter.

Food Chains

Many of the algae that live in water are so tiny that we can see them only through a microscope. Yet these algae form the basis of food chains for everything from one-celled animals to giant whales. If the algae die, so do all the other organisms in the food chains.

Like all other living things, algae need food to survive. Unlike people and animals, they make their own food, in a process called photosynthesis. Light is needed for photosynthesis. If wastes containing high amounts of suspended soil and other sediment enters a waterway, photosynthesis may cease. The suspended sediment limits the amount of light penetrating the water. The sediment can also smother fish eggs and animals that live along the bottom of a waterway.

Heavy metals, pesticides and other chemicals can be lethal to aquatic organisms. In 1969, following an accidental pesticide spill from a chemical factory in Frankfurt, West Germany, millions of fish in the Rhine River were killed. But even seemingly insignificant amounts of chemicals can create havoc. Washing out an "empty" pesticide container in a small pond or creek can dump enough chemicals into the water to kill or inhibit the growth of many species.

Another problem is that fat-soluble chemicals become concentrated to dangerous levels in the bodies of organisms. Oysters have been shown to remove DDT from water and concentrate it in their tissues at a level 70,000 times greater than that in the water! If a fish feeds on such oysters, the DDT accumulates in its body. If an eagle or other predator eats the fish, the DDT is passed on. If it eats many contaminated fish, the build-up of pesticide in its body may be sufficient to kill the predator outright. Or it may cause other harm, such as preventing the predator's eggs from developing properly.

A 1989 study of fish caught in the Great Lakes found that 90% contained levels of toxic chemicals such as DDT and PCBs that were dangerous to wildlife; 25% contained levels dangerous to humans.

People often ingest dangerous chemicals when they eat contaminated fish or shellfish. One of the most tragic cases occurred in Minamata, Japan, during the 1950s. Hundreds of townspeople died and thousands more suffered permanent brain damage as a result of mercury poisoning. The problem was traced to contaminated fish and shellfish caught in the nearby sea. Wastewaters from a plastics factory had been regularly dumped into the sea. The wastes contained mercury, which moved up the food chain and accumulated in the animals' bodies. Then unsuspecting people ate the animals.

Eutrophication

Sewage, fertilizers, silt and some other wastes are rich in nutrients—such as nitrogen and phosphate—needed for plant growth. As the concentration of these nutrients increases in a lake or other waterway, algae and other plants grow much more rapidly than normal. Gradually, this depletes the oxygen supply that is so necessary for the decomposition of wastes by bacteria. Lowered oxygen supplies also affect fish. Species such as trout, bass and perch die. They are replaced by species such as carp and buffalo fish, which do not require as much oxygen. In time, as oxygen levels drop lower and lower, even these fish will be unable to survive.

Massive concentrations of algae, called algal blooms, are the most common signal of eutrophication. In 1988, a foul-smelling, yellow-brown slick formed by a microscopic algae began killing salmon off the coast of Sweden. Currents carried the slick northward. Soon it threatened salmon-rearing industries along the Norwegian coast. Huge numbers of cages containing young salmon were towed deep into the Norwegian fjords to save the fish. Marine biologists were quite certain of the underlying cause of this bloom: excessive amounts of nutrients dumped into the ocean by human activities.

In 1989, a vast algal bloom spread over hundreds of square miles of the Adriatic Sea, forming a gelatinous "soup" up to 40 feet (12 meters) thick in places. It killed fish and other marine life, broke fishermen's nets and covered bathers with slime. The algal populations were highest near mouths of rivers and city sewage outlets, indicating that land sources

One of the most tragic incidents of mercury poisoning occured in the 1950s in Minamata, Japan. Hundreds died and thousands were permanently brain damaged as a result of eating tainted fish.

were a major cause of the bloom. Indeed, one of the rivers that empties into the Adriatic Sea in this area is Italy's Po River. Each year, it carries 18,000 tons of phosphates and 135,000 tons of nitrates into the sea.

Additional evidence that blooms are caused by human activities comes from the Inland Sea (Seto-naikai) of Japan. This is a long, narrow body of water surrounded by three large islands. Among the harbor cities on the sea are Hiroshima, Kobe and Osaka. Algal blooms became increasingly common in the sea, increasing from 40 a year in 1965 to more than 300 a year by 1973. In 1972, pollution controls were introduced. Their purpose was to cut by 50% the amount of nutrients entering the sea. It worked: the frequency of algal blooms in the Inland Sea has been declining steadily since 1975.

Human Health

Numerous diseases may be spread through polluted water. This is a particularly serious problem in developing countries where poverty is widespread and sanitation facilities may be minimal or nonexistent. For instance, in Latin America alone, the homeless include some 21 million orphaned and abandoned children who live on the streets. Their lack of access to even the most basic sanitary facilities creates health problems both for themselves and for the populations as a whole.

One of the deadliest waterborne diseases is cholera. This disease is caused by bacteria. It is generally spread through water or food that is contaminated with the feces or urine of people who have the disease. Without prompt treatment, the victim often dies.

Two other diseases that are usually spread by water and food contaminated with human wastes are typhoid fever, caused by a bacterium, and hepatitis A, caused by a virus. In the United States, the most frequently reported waterborne disease is gastroenteritis. This is actually a group of diseases caused by various bacteria, viruses and protozoa. Its symptoms include nausea, vomiting and diarrhea—symptoms that are also associated with colds and other illnesses not related to drinking water.

Chemical contaminants may also cause serious health problems. In industrialized countries, industrial and mining operations are the major source of these pollutants. In the United States, the organic chemical and plastic industries are the largest sources; metal finishing plants and the iron and steel industries are also large contributors.

Chlorinated compounds, formed when chlorine is used to treat industrial and municipal wastewaters, cause cancer. Lead damages the nervous system and causes birth defects and learning disabilities. Cadmium causes liver damage and high blood pressure. Nitrates—primarily from agricultural runoff—can interfere with the blood's ability to carry oxygen.

Recreation

Lakes, rivers and oceans are widely used for recreation. But when the water becomes polluted with sewage and other wastes, swimming and other recreational activities may be banned. Boating may become unsafe because of excessive plant growth. Fishing may be prohibited because of dangerous levels of toxic substances in marine life. Skin diving would be less enjoyable if pollution limits visibility and kills sea life.

Economic Costs

Treating wastewater to remove pollutants is costly. Building and operating water treatment facilities costs millions of dollars. Even costlier, however, is not treating this water. Pollution of surface waters and groundwater limits water supplies—at a time when demands for drinking, agriculture and other uses are increasing. Pollution threatens the commercial fishing industry, which provides thousands of jobs. Pollution leads to illnesses requiring medical care. It harms resort communities, sports shops and other businesses dependent on swimmers, water-skiers and other recreational users of waterways. It damages ships, bridges and other water equipment. Cleanup efforts, which might have been avoided by preventive measures, are generally difficult and very expensive.

8

TREATING
WASTEWATERS

For most of human history, people depended on natural processes to cleanse wastewater. As sewage flowed—or was dumped—into waterways, bacteria decomposed organic wastes. Alkaline substances neutralized acids. Sunlight broke down certain compounds.

But as human populations grew and produced ever larger quantities of sewage, natural systems became overwhelmed. They could not break down the wastes fast enough. Waterways became ever more polluted. Fish and other organisms living in the waterways died. People who depended on the waterways for drinking water supplies became ill. Catastrophic epidemics occurred.

Today, it is widely recognized that to avoid health hazards and environmental damage, sewage must be treated to remove pollutants. There are, however, wide differences in how sewage is treated among communities and even among countries. In many parts of the world, a lack of money to build treatment facilities means that millions of gallons of sewage is dumped untreated into rivers and oceans. At the other end of the spectrum, elaborate sewer systems carry sewage to technologically advanced waste treatment plants.

Sewer Systems

Some sewer systems carry all forms of wastewater, including both sewage from buildings and storm runoff. This may

Opposite page:
Wastewater that has been treated effectively can be put to further use. Here, a metal arm scrapes floating debris off the surface of wastewater that is proceeding toward clarifying facilities at a wastewater treatment plant.

75

SEPTIC TANKS

A family that lives in a sparsely populated area may not be connected to a sewer system. They need another method to treat wastewater. The most common method is a septic system. This consists of a septic tank and a soil absorption field.

Wastewater flows through a pipe from the family's home into the septic tank. This is a watertight container made of metal or concrete. It is buried in the ground a short distance from the home. Solid matter settles to the bottom of the tank, where anaerobic bacteria (bacteria that can live without oxygen) digest organic matter. The sludge that forms must periodically be pumped out of the tank.

Liquid wastes gradually pass out of the upper portion of the septic tank through perforated pipes and into the surrounding soil. Bacteria in the soil decompose some of the wastes. Some undissolved nutrients cling to soil particles and become available to plants, which can absorb them through the roots.

Septic systems must be carefully placed, to be certain that water is purified before it seeps into groundwater or reaches lakes and streams. Unfortunately, many septic systems are poorly sited or poorly built. Many are not well maintained. As a result, septic systems are a major source of groundwater pollution.

present a problem following heavy rainstorms. Many treatment plants are unable to handle the large volumes of water produced at such times. Some of the wastewater must then bypass the plants and enter waterways untreated.

Many newer sewer systems consist of two separate pathways: one for residential and industrial wastes, the other for runoff. This has two advantages. When the volume of wastewater becomes too great, runoff can be emptied into a waterway without treatment while the more serious sewage can still be treated. Also, because runoff generally does not carry as many pollutants, it can sometimes be released into the environment after fewer treatment steps.

Three Stages of Treatment

There are three standard treatment stages: primary, secondary and tertiary. About 30% of the impurities and contaminants in wastewater are removed by primary treatment. This is largely a mechanical process. The sewage passes through a series of screens, grit chambers and sedimentation tanks. The screens prevent the passage of leaves, trash and other large solid objects. These objects may be buried in landfills. Or they may be shredded, then returned to the wastewater to be treated elsewhere in the treatment plant.

In the grit chambers, the wastewater flows at a rate slow enough for grit (sand, small stones, etc.) to fall to the bottom. Next, the wastewater flows to sedimentation tanks, where it remains for several hours. This allows much of the silt and other suspended matter to settle to the bottom of the tanks. The accumulation of solids at the bottom of the tanks is called primary sludge. It is removed by scrapers and pumps.

Secondary treatment is primarily a biological process. Its purpose is to decompose organic material still in the wastewater. This is done by adding aerobic bacteria. The bacteria need air to function. Therefore, all secondary treatment mixes air with the wastewater. In one method, called the activated-sludge process, wastewater enters an aeration tank where air is bubbled through the wastewater. This encourages the growth of the aerobic bacteria. The concentrations of bacteria are so great that a residue called floc, or activated

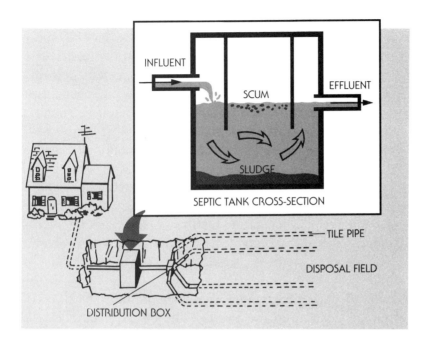

INFLUENT

SCUM

EFFLUENT

SLUDGE

SEPTIC TANK CROSS-SECTION

TILE PIPE

DISPOSAL FIELD

DISTRIBUTION BOX

sludge, forms. After several hours, the mixture of wastewater and activated sludge is pumped into secondary sedimentation tanks. Here the activated sludge settles to the bottom. Because it contains huge numbers of helpful bacteria, some of it is returned to the aeration tank to treat incoming wastewater.

An alternative method is the trickling filter. It consists of a bed of coarse rocks or plastic lattices on which aerobic bacteria grow. The wastewater trickles through the bed, allowing time for the bacteria to feed off the organic wastes, and forming a muck called secondary sludge.

The liquid, or effluent, that remains may now be disinfected, usually with chlorine. This destroys disease-causing bacteria and reduces odors. At this point, about 85% of the pollutants have been removed. This was once considered sufficient for most municipal wastewaters, and the effluent was released into waterways.

Because of ever-growing populations plus the increasing amounts of toxic chemicals being dumped in wastewater, many industrialized nations now require some tertiary treatment. These processes remove dissolved materials such as phosphates, nitrates and heavy metals.

Many factories have their own wastewater treatment plants. In some cases, these are basically the same as municipal plants. But if the factories produce toxic wastes, the wastewater may require special treatment before it is discharged. For example, metal factories often use special processes to reduce the concentration of chemicals such as cyanide. In contrast, food processors do not generate toxic chemicals but do need to reduce the amount of organic matter in their wastewater.

The cost of water treatment rises as the treatment becomes more complex. Yet even the most advanced treatments may not remove all the toxic materials added to water by today's industries. Pesticides and heavy metals are special problems because they tend to pass unaffected through treatment plants.

Every day, some communities dump millions of gallons of sewage sludge into the oceans. The thick, black goo kills everything in its path. Some creatures are killed almost instantly. Others die slow deaths: the fins of fish rot, the feeding systems of clams become clogged with poisons, and so on. A "dead sea" is created; only bacteria and a few species of worms live in the area.

This environmental devastation is unnecessary. Sludge produced during the various treatment stages can be treated and disposed of in safer, perhaps even beneficial ways. Much depends on the source and contents of the sludge. Sludges resulting from the processing of wastewaters from food processors, paper mills, nuclear power plants and residential communities are very, very different.

One practice is to dry the sludge out and then incinerate it. If the sludge contains heavy metals, these will be concentrated in the ash, presenting a landfill problem.

Another practice is digestion using anaerobic bacteria. These bacteria live and grow without oxygen. The sludge is pumped into an airless tank containing the bacteria. Over the course of several weeks, the bacteria digest the sludge. During the process, they produce methane. This gas can be used to heat the treatment plant and to produce some of its power. It can even be used to warm the digestion tank, helping to speed the bacterial processes.

Digested sludge can be disposed of in a landfill. Or it can be used to condition soil. It is often used to reclaim strip-mined lands and other barren areas. If the digested sludge is dried at very high temperatures, all disease-causing organisms are killed. Unless it contains significant concentrations of heavy metals or other hazardous wastes, it can then be used as a fertilizer on farms and gardens.

Natural Sewage Systems

Instead of building conventional secondary and tertiary treatment facilities, some communities are using Mother Nature. They use bacteria, algae, sunlight and green plants to treat wastewater.

One example of a natural system can be seen in Arcata, California. The California environmental agency told Arcata and two neighboring towns that they were discharging inadequately treated wastewater into Humboldt Bay. The state wanted to build a $56 million sewage plant in Arcata, but town residents objected. Instead, Arcata Marsh was created—for less than $700,000.

Arcata Marsh has 175 acres (70 hectares) of man-made wetlands. Wastewater receives primary treatment in the city's sewage treatment plant, then flows into 50 acres (20 hectares) of oxidation ponds. Here, biological decomposition takes place. Next, the effluent flows through marshes planted with bulrushes and cattails. Bacteria and other microorganisms living on the plant roots feed on organic matter in the effluent. Equally important, bulrushes and cattails—like many marsh plants—have the ability to remove toxic chemicals and metals from the water. Basically, they perform the same function as tertiary treatment in traditional facilities. After the water leaves the treatment plant, it takes about two months for it to meander through the marshes. By the time the effluent leaves Arcata Marsh and flows into Humboldt Bay, it is actually cleaner than the water already in the bay.

Ducks, egrets, sandpipers and other birds have settled into Arcata Marsh. Otters, mice and muskrats live there. Fish and shellfish populate some of the waters. And human visitors find the habitat an attractive place to stroll and bird-watch.

9

REDUCING WASTE

Everyone has heard parents and grandparents talk about "the good old days." Well, there *were* some good things about those days, particularly when it comes to limiting wastes.

It wasn't too many years ago that people would buy soft drinks and beer in refillable bottles. When the bottles were empty, people would take them back to the beverage distributor, who would ship them to the bottling plant to be washed and refilled.

It wasn't too many years ago that fountain pens were treasured gifts, to be used for a lifetime. All pens were reusable. When they were empty, the person simply refilled them from a bottle of ink.

It wasn't too many years ago that parents used cloth diapers for their babies. When the baby was changed, the diaper was washed. It was used and washed over and over again, until the child no longer needed diapers. Then the diaper was used for the next baby. If the diaper was too worn, it was used as a rag for cleaning chores, torn into strips to hold up tomato plants or put to some other use.

These practices are still common in many parts of the world. But in the United States and some other industrialized nations, they have been largely replaced by convenience products. As we face a growing waste crisis, however, products and habits of "the good old days" are making a comeback.

Opposite page:
There are many methods by which individuals can help to ease the solid waste crisis. Re-using shopping bags, razor blades and cloth towels are only a few simple ways to become less wasteful.

People are beginning to realize that the best way to limit waste problems is to produce fewer wastes.

Less waste preserves scarce landfills. Less waste lessens the need for large, costly incinerators. Less waste is the surest way to cut pollution, thus reducing risks to health and the environment. This is particularly true for hazardous wastes. Less waste also conserves valuable resources. For example, sterilizing and refilling a glass bottle uses much less energy than making a new bottle from recycled materials. The energy savings is even greater when compared with making a new bottle from raw materials.

Reduction can even be profitable, especially when the money saved by avoiding disposal fees is taken into account.

Opportunities to reduce the generation of wastes are everywhere. Taking advantage of these opportunities will prevent future environmental problems and go far toward helping us solve the waste crisis.

How Industries Can Reduce Wastes

Companies can take several different approaches to reduce or eliminate wastes. When a broad range of projects are undertaken, dramatic reductions can occur. General Dynamics reduced hazardous waste discharges by 61% between 1985 and 1989. From 1984 to 1985, two Du Pont divisions reported 50% and 35% reductions of hazardous waste production. Monsanto reported a 20% reduction from 1982 to 1984. Olin Corporation reported a 34% drop from 1981 to 1985.

Such reductions result in significant savings of money. Companies that undertake waste reduction find that the process pays for itself relatively quickly. ARCO found that a series of waste-reduction changes at its refinery complex in Los Angeles reduced the volume of wastes from about 12,000 tons a year in the early 1980s to about 3,400 tons in 1989. As a result, ARCO saved approximately $2 million a year in disposal costs. Ciba-Geigy invested $300,000 in process changes and recovery equipment at its plant in Toms River, New Jersey. The investment reduced disposal costs by over $1.8 million between 1985 and 1988.

Changing Raw Materials

One way to reduce hazardous wastes is to minimize the use of raw materials that contain toxic chemicals. For example, water-based solvents can be used instead of toxic organic solvents. In 1990, General Dynamics substituted water-based cleaners and terpene hydrocarbons for a solvent blend containing the toxins naphtha, perchlorethylene and methylene chloride. The switch was expected to reduce hazardous wastes by 20 to 25 tons a year.

Changing Production

Another approach is to change production technology, equipment and procedures. New, low-waste technology can be installed in a factory. Or current equipment can be modified to include improvements.

Mechanical techniques can be used instead of toxic organic solvents to clean metal surfaces. In mid-1989, General Dynamics switched from cleaning adhesive fasteners with a methylene chloride solution to a mechanically agitated, non-solvent system. Within six months, this project eliminated 11 tons of hazardous wastes.

In Sweden, pulp and paper mills use new technologies to decrease the use of chlorine in bleaching paper. This in turn reduces the release of dioxin into nearby waters. Some mills are also testing alternatives to chlorine bleach, such as hydrogen peroxide and ozone.

During the manufacture of metals, plastics and paper, large amounts of scrap are often produced. The scrap can be fed directly back into the manufacturing process or into a related process. For example, scrap produced during the stamping of steel parts for automobiles is melted and cast into engine blocks. Scrap produced during the manufacture of polyvinyl chloride (PVC) automobile parts such as dashboards and seat covers is reground, melted and mixed with virgin PVC. Paper mill trimmings are repulped and made into new paper.

Changing Products and Packaging

Some products can be redesigned or reformulated so that manufacturing them generates less waste. For example, combining laundry detergent and bleach into one product reduces packaging. In some countries, Procter & Gamble has introduced a detergent in a refillable, reusable container. Shoppers buy the bottled product once, then buy pouches of concentrates to mix with water in the original container.

Packaging can be made more efficient. Products that are excessively packaged are obvious targets. But major savings can also be achieved elsewhere. One method is to reduce the thickness of the package. As a result of this and other changes, today's aluminum beverage can uses 30% less metal than its 1972 counterpart. And a redesigned Crisco Oil bottle holds the same amount of oil with 28% less plastic.

Wastes are reduced when disposable packaging is replaced by reusable packaging. The Schroeder Milk Company of Minnesota now provides milk in returnable high-density polyethylene (HDPE) plastic containers. Each container can be used 50 times. Thus, only one reusable container enters the waste stream instead of 50 single-use containers. Indeed, when the jugs are worn out, Schroeder recycles them, giving them yet another life.

Rehrig Pacific of California created the Castle Crate. Made of HDPE, the Castle Crate holds 8 two-liter soft drink bottles. It can be used for shipping and as a display in the grocery store. It has a 7- to 12-year life span. Each time it carries soft drinks, it eliminates the need for cardboard shipping boxes and corrugated paperboard filler.

Changing Wastes to Resources

Another approach to waste reduction is to change a potential waste into something useful. For example, instead of allowing heat to escape up a smokestack and into the atmosphere, many factories use the heat to produce steam. The steam is used to run an electric generator. This decreases the amount of electricity that the factory must buy from an outside source. Similarly, pulp and paper mills have long burned bark and wood refuse to yield useful energy.

Sometimes, the waste from one process can serve as a raw material for another process. Meridian National, a steel-processing company in Ohio, uses sulfuric acid to remove scale from steel sheets. Ferrous sulfate compounds are formed, which Meridian sells to manufacturers of magnetic tape. Leftovers from milling wheat, crushing soybeans, slaughtering animals and other food processing activities provide 43 million tons of livestock feed annually.

Even the new science of genetic engineering can aid in waste reduction. Genetic engineering is the process of inserting a gene from one organism into another organism, for the purpose of changing one of the latter's characteristics. This procedure has enabled scientists at the University of Kentucky to develop a way to change a waste produced by cheesemakers into a substance that can be used by breweries.

During the cheese-making process, a liquid called whey is formed. Traditionally, the whey has been discarded. However, whey contains sugar lactose, which can be changed into alcohol. The brewery industry has long used the yeast *Saccharomyces cerevisiae* to break down the sugar maltose, found in barley and other cereal grains. The yeast changes the maltose into alcohol and carbon dioxide. It cannot change lactose into alcohol, however. It lacks the necessary genes. The University of Kentucky scientists transferred the genes from other yeast species to *S. cerevisiae*. Now the yeast can break down the lactose in whey. This gave the brewery industry a new source of raw materials—and eliminated a major waste of the cheese-making industry.

How Consumers Can Reduce Solid Wastes

Every day, home and office wastebaskets are filled with junk mail. This includes advertising circulars, catalogs, appeals for donations and other unrequested printed matter. Much of the mail is not even opened by recipients; it goes directly from mailbox to wastebasket to town dump. People can reduce the amount of junk mail they receive. One way is by writing to companies that send the material and asking to be removed from their mailing lists. In the United States, people can also contact the Direct Marketing Association in New York City and request to have their names removed from mailing lists. This may reduce the amount of junk mail delivered to a home by up to 50%.

Perhaps the most critical decisions regarding waste reduction are made in stores. People can significantly cut the amount of wastes they generate by making wise shopping decisions. Purchasing products with long lifetimes instead of competing products with short lives saves on wastes—and usually saves money, too. Examples of such products include longer lasting tires and long-life, energy-efficient light bulbs. Repairing items—from clothes to appliances—is another way to expand product lifetimes. Donating or selling used items also helps. Charities and consignment shops are eager to accept used items in good condition.

Most disposable products are designed to be used once and then discarded. They can be replaced by reusable products. A school lunch carried in a plastic sandwich box instead of plastic or waxed paper sandwich bags saves some 200 bags a year. Using a hand towel or sponge instead of paper towels easily saves several rolls of towels a year.

Packaging

Whenever possible, consumers should buy products without packaging. Of course, in many cases this is not possible. Even then, however, consumers can make important choices. They can avoid excessive packaging. For instance, cough medicine must obviously be packaged in a bottle. But the bottle does not have to be placed in a box. The box does not have to be shrink wrapped. A plastic spoon does not have to be included with the bottle.

Type of packaging is important, too. Packaging that is made from recycled materials and that can be recycled is preferred. For example, glass bottles are environmentally smarter than containers made from multiple layers of different plastics, such as squeezeable ketchup and mustard bottles.

Package size is another consideration. A large food container uses less packaging than two smaller containers. For example, a 16-ounce can uses 40% less metal than two 8-ounce cans.

Consumers can reduce waste by carrying their own, reusable shopping bags. This is much wiser than using a store's paper or plastic bags, even if these can be recycled.

Hazardous Wastes

Toxic products commonly used in homes can often be replaced by nontoxic alternatives. Some replacements are homemade mixtures; others are sold in stores or by mail-order companies.

Many household cleaning jobs can be done with soap and water instead of strong cleaning solvents. Clogged drains can usually be cleared with baking soda and vinegar, flushed with boiling water. Furniture and floors can be polished with commercial products that use lemon oil or beeswax in a mineral oil base—or with a homemade mixture of one part lemon juice to two parts vegetable oil. Ants can be controlled by sprinkling boric acid, bone meal or talcum powder across their trails.

Water Conservation

Most water used by industries and homes is taken from a river or other waterway or from an underground aquifer. It is used once, then discharged as wastewater. The wastewater must be treated if it is not to harm the environment. The greater the amount of wastewater produced, the greater the demands on treatment facilities. And, the greater the demands on water supplies. Both are important and growing problems in many places. Freshwater supplies are dwindling or insufficient to meet the needs of increasing populations. Wastewater treatment plants cannot properly handle the massive amounts of water flowing into them. These problems can be lessened by reducing water intake and discharge. This can be done by both industries and consumers.

One growing industrial practice is reusing water. Industries that reuse water several times before discharging it decrease the amount of fresh water they withdraw from rivers and other waterways. They also decrease the quantity of water that needs to be treated before it can be discharged back into waterways.

In Sweden, the pulp and paper industry accounts for 80% of industrial water use. After the country established strict water-pollution standards, the industry developed ways to

Do you buy the hammer hung on a rack—or the same type of hammer packaged in a plastic blister pack? Do you pick the oranges you want from a pile of loose oranges—or those shrink-wrapped on a plastic tray. Do you choose jelly in a glass jar that can later be recycled—or jelly in a container that cannot be recycled?

As a consumer, you are given many choices when you go shopping. Making the right choices can often help protect the environment and limit the amount of wastes you produce.

You may be only one of thousands or even millions of people in your community. But your shopping habits do make a difference. As the saying goes, if you're not part of the solution, you're part of the problem.

1. Say NO to overpackaged products. Choose comparable products with minimal packaging that can be recycled—or with no packaging at all.

2. Say NO to products in single-serving containers. Choose comparable products sold in bulk.

3. Say NO to disposables. Choose comparable products that can be reused or recycled.

4. Say NO to paper and plastic bags used in stores. Carry a reusable bag when you shop.

reuse water in its mills. Instead of continually drawing in fresh water, the same water was reused over and over again. The Swedish Ministry of Agriculture reported that between the early 1960s and the mid-1970s, the pulp and paper industry cut its water use in half—at the same time that it doubled production. This means there was actually a fourfold increase in water-use efficiency during that time period.

An Armco steel mill in Kansas City, Missouri, uses water 16 times before discharging it. As a result, it uses only 12 cubic yards (9 cubic meters) of water for each ton of steel it produces. In comparison, many other steel mills use up to 260 cubic yards (200 cubic meters) of water per ton of steel produced.

Consumers can take a variety of steps to reduce the amount of sewage they produce. Each time a typical American toilet is flushed, it uses about 5 gallons (19 liters) of water. But there are toilets on the market that use 3.5 gallons (13 liters) or less per flush. A conventional showerhead uses about 5 gallons (19 liters) of water a minute. Thus, even a short 3-minute shower can produce as much as 15 gallons (57 liters) of wastewater. Installing a water-saving showerhead can cut water flow in half—yet give the bather the same feeling and rinsing action as a water-guzzling showerhead.

Encouraging Reduction

A number of actions can be taken by legislators, business management and consumers to encourage waste reduction.

Government agencies can create grant programs for people who develop low-waste technologies. Tax incentives can be provided to businesses that use these technologies.

Governments can also publicize and support effective waste reduction programs. In Canada and the United States there are more than a dozen waste exchange programs that match manufacturers who generate useful wastes with manufacturers who can use those wastes as raw materials.

Some places have used laws to enforce waste reduction. In Denmark, Norway and West Germany, government agencies may ban packaging that cannot easily be refilled or recycled. Florence, Italy, has banned the sale of plastic food containers. Some U.S. communities have adopted building codes that require the installation of efficient plumbing fixtures in new and renovated buildings.

Tougher pollution discharge regulations often spur the development of techniques that produce fewer wastes. So does higher costs for energy, water and raw materials.

Industrial managers can encourage employees to think of waste reduction as part of their everyday activities. They can reward workers who suggest ways to reduce wastes.

Many of these steps depend on support from the general public. By choosing products that produce fewer wastes and are less destructive to the environment, consumers send an important message to manufacturers. The same message can be communicated in letters and even in person. Write to manufacturers to say you won't buy their product until it is in less wasteful packaging. Tell grocers you don't want your vegetables in a plastic foam tray wrapped in plastic. Such actions can be extremely effective. When Swedish consumers stopped buying pure white paper products because they linked these with dioxin and other toxic pollutants, Swedish pulp and paper mills began testing new ways to bleach paper.

At all levels of a society, there is a need for new attitudes towards wastes. Everyone—from government officials to business leaders to teachers to parents and young children—can work to change people's attitudes.

10
RECYCLING

Almost everything we use—from the paper we write on to the vehicles we ride in—may contain recycled materials. Electric motors may contain recycled copper. Cereal boxes are often made of recycled paper. Automobile batteries can contain recycled lead. Television sets may contain recycled zinc. The aluminum beverage cans on the supermarket shelves are often made from cans that sat on those same shelves a few months ago. Woolen coats on department store racks may be made from woolen coats that were sold from those same racks several years earlier.

Recycling is the most effective way to reduce the amount of wastes we produce. It prevents useful materials from being landfilled or burned, preserves our waste disposal capacity and cuts pollution. It conserves energy and natural resources. The savings can be enormous. Using recycled aluminum instead of aluminum ore cuts air pollution by 95%, water pollution by 97% and energy use by an average of 95%. Substituting scrap steel for virgin materials cuts air pollution 85%, water pollution 76%, energy use an average of 63% and water use 40%. Making paper from recycled materials cuts air pollution 74%, water pollution 35%, energy use more than 70% and water use 58%.

Recycling also is cost effective, especially when the avoided costs of disposal are considered. In the first two years that the

Opposite page:
Recycling solid materials such as bottles, cans, paper products and tires has become the single most effective way to reduce the amount of wastes we produce.

Coca-Cola Company recycled paper at its Atlanta, Georgia, headquarters, it collected approximately 25 tons of paper, newsprint and corrugated containers. It made $26,000 in profits from the recycling program. In 1988, AT&T made $190,000 on the 3,800 tons of used office paper it collected.

While some consumers keep a record of how much money they saved—or even earned—by recycling, others keep track of the resources they saved. Cravath, Swaine & Moore, a New York City law firm, uses 70 million sheets of paper and nearly 16,000 legal pads every year. It began an intense recycling program in July 1990. Everything from visitors' passes and file cards to photocopying paper went into 1,500 recycling trays distributed to the staff. In less than three months, it recycled enough paper to replace virgin paper produced from 680 trees! And instead of paying to have the waste paper carted away, the firm collected $12 to $15 a ton for it.

Recycling is a multi-step process. It begins with the separation and collection of recyclable materials. The materials are transported to scrap processors. Here, in large yards and plants, the wastes are sorted, segregated and prepared for shipment to industrial users. These users include paper mills, rubber manufacturers, steel mills, aluminum smelters, textile factories and hundreds of other industries that use recycled raw materials to make new products. Finally, the new products are sold to businesses that market them to consumers.

The public has the key role. We begin and end the process. As individuals and communities, we begin the process by saving and collecting recyclable materials. We end the process by buying and using products made from recycled materials, rather than products made from virgin materials. There must be a market for the recycled products, or manufacturers will not make those products. As one county official said, "You can collect all you want, but you can only recycle what you can market."

Some countries have advanced recycling programs. In Japan and the Netherlands, half or more of all waste paper was being recycled by 1990. In contrast, less than a third of the waste paper in the United States and Great Britain was

TIRE FIRE

At a dump in Hagersville, Ontario, used tires were stacked in piles as high as a three-story building. Some 14 million tires were stored on the 11-acre (4.5-hectare) site. During the night of February 11–12, 1990, they began to burn. They burned for 17 days, at temperatures hot enough to melt steel. By the time firefighters had put the fire out, most of the 14 million tires had been consumed. It was the largest tire fire ever in North America.

The fire released thousands of pounds of toxic chemicals into the environment. About 158,000 gallons (598,000 liters) of oil, formed as the rubber melted, were collected and processed at a nearby refinery. Thousands of additional gallons soaked into the ground. Millions of pounds of toxic gases dispersed into the atmosphere.

Thousands of tire dumps litter the North American landscape. In the United States alone, such dumps hold an estimated 2.5 billion to 3 billion used tires. Each year, another 280 million tires are added to the piles.

Tires do not have to sit in huge, unsightly piles. It is possible to recycle them. Some tires can be recycled the old-fashioned way, by retreading. This involves removing the worn tread and replacing it with new

tread. Some tires can be broken up into raw materials that can be used in new rubber and plastic products. Tires can be shredded and used as fuel in cement kilns, paper manufacturing facilities and electric power plants. They can be ground and mixed with asphalt to produce paving materials for roads and airport runways. Whole tires can be used for playground equipment, as buffers at marine docks and in reef construction.

Recycling tires is not common in North America, however. The primary reason is economics. The machinery needed to grind rubber into small particles for reprocessing into new products is expensive. Burning tires as fuel requires expensive equipment to handle air emissions. Although rubber-based asphalt lasts longer, it is more expensive to produce than concrete.

being recycled. In the Netherlands, 53% of all glass was recycled in 1990. In the United States, only 10% was being recycled.

Until recently, most collection of recyclable materials in the United States was done through private organizations. For example, the aluminum industry set up a network of aluminum collection and processing centers. Scouting groups organized newspaper collections. But as recycling has become increasingly important, communities have begun to operate large-scale collection systems. These take various forms. Some communities have curbside pickup of materials that have been separated by homeowners. A community may even provide householders with special containers for the separated wastes. Other communities have drop-off centers. These centers may be as simple as a shed at the local landfill where people or machines sort recyclables. Or they may be as elaborate as the "theme center" in Tallahassee, Florida, which was designed to look like a fort on the old American frontier.

Closed and Open Loops

Products made from recycled materials may or may not resemble the original material. In some cases, a material is used over and over again for the same purpose. This is sometimes called a closed-loop process. For example, when aluminum cans are recycled they are melted down and the molten metal is cast into new cans. When glass bottles are recycled, they are turned into new glass containers. This can usually be done over and over again. It limits the need to use virgin materials to make aluminum or glass containers.

Other recycling programs do not close the loop. Rather, one type of item is turned into another type of item. Plastic fast-food packages made of polystyrene are collected and used in the manufacture of park benches, combs and other items—but not to make new fast-food packages. This means that manufacturers of polystyrene fast-food packages must always use virgin materials to make more polystyrene for their products. Environmentalists are unhappy about this continual depletion of natural resources. Jeanne Wirka, a solid waste policy analyst at the Environmental Action Foundation, commented, "We will have achieved little if in recycling we do not reduce the demand for virgin material."

Recycling Paper

In addition to the energy and other savings noted above, recycling paper produces less toxic wastes than making paper from wood pulp. It uses fewer chemicals and requires less bleaching. However, waste paper must be de-inked. The ink, plus clay, fiber fragments and other materials end up in sludge. In some cases, this is buried in hazardous waste landfills. In other cases, it is nontoxic and can be used as a soil conditioner.

More than 25% of the paper used by people in the United States was being recovered by the start of the 1990s. As collection systems expand, the percentage is expected to increase.

There are several types of paper. For recycling to be successful, these must be separated because different types of paper lend themselves to making different types of new products.

Newspapers form one category. They have long been among the most commonly recycled materials. They are the main kind of paper collected from homes. They are used primarily to make new newsprint and paperboard. Food boxes with gray interiors are generally made from recycled newsprint.

High-grade paper is a second category. It includes white typing and writing papers, index cards and computer print-outs. It can be used to make printing, writing and tissue papers.

Corrugated cardboard and other paperboard make up the third major category. They are the largest source of waste paper; in 1989 about 50% of the corrugated boxes discarded in the United States were recovered for recycling. Many businesses that generate large amounts of paperboard have their own baling equipment to prepare the paper for mills. Paperboard is recycled to make various kinds of paperboard.

Other papers—envelopes, blueprint paper, colored papers and so on—can be recycled, though this may need to be done separately. They contain contaminants such as glues and dyes. For example, telephone books are difficult to recycle because the glue used to bind the books sticks to the pulping equipment and the yellow dye used on the pages is hard to remove. Many outdated telephone books from the United States are shipped to Asian countries such as Taiwan and India, where they are used to make roofing felt, panel board and other building products.

Glossy papers, such as those used in many magazines, have long, strong fibers. But they contain clay. In the past, this has made it difficult or uneconomic to recycle glossy paper. A

MENACE ON THE MNGEWENI

Recycling programs should help protect human health and the environment—not harm them. Unfortunately, without strict regulations, recyclers may be significant polluters. Such was the case at a mercury reprocessing facility operated by Britain's Thor Chemicals at Cato Ridge, South Africa. Mercury wastes were shipped to the facility by Thor clients in other countries. For example, at the beginning of the 1990s, a division of American Cyanamid, a company located in New Jersey, was sending Thor Chemicals some 10 tons of wastes each year. The wastes were produced during the manufacture of heat-resistant hoses, engine seals and other products.

A significant amount of the mercury that arrived at Cato Ridge ended up in the environment. It contaminated the Mngeweni River, which supplies water to rural villages downstream from the facility. Sediment samples taken by Greenpeace, an international environmental organization, found mercury contamination as high as 1,760 parts per million. This is 8,600 times the limit established by the U.S. government to define hazardous waste!

process invented by a German company, Steinbeis and Consorten, has solved this problem. By 1990, Steinbeis was using the process to make about 15% of the duplicating paper produced in Germany.

Paper cannot be recycled indefinitely. Each time paper is repulped, the cellulose fibers are weakened and shortened. Thus better quality recycled paper contains a significant percentage of virgin pulp.

The statement "made with recycled paper" is sometimes misleading, say environmentalists. They point out that much of the paper that is labeled "recycled" actually contains 50% or more virgin pulp, combined with pre-consumer wastes: industrial scrap such as mill wastes and envelope clippings. It is not made from post-consumer wastes—that is, paper used in homes and offices. Manufacturing leftovers have long been reclaimed and used. Post-consumer paper, however, has generally ended up in landfills and incinerators.

Recycling Plastics

Plastics recycling is a relatively young industry. In 1989, only 1% of plastic wastes in the United States were being recycled. This percentage is expected to increase as processing technologies are developed. One major problem with trying to recycle plastics has been how to efficiently sort a mixture of plastics into single resins. Mixed plastic is being used to make park benches, trash containers, fence posts and other items. But separating the different types would expand their recyclability.

Generally, plastics with a short useful life, such as a soft-drink container, are converted into plastics with a long life span, such as irrigation piping. The soft-drink containers and other packaging generally cannot be recycled into new packaging. The U.S. Food and Drug Administration requires that packaging be free of contamination. This means the packaging must be sterilized. However, during recycling, plastics are not exposed to enough heat to sterilize them.

The most commonly recycled plastic at the present time is polyethylene terephthalate (PET). Most plastic soft-drink bottles are made of PET. They are reprocessed to produce

THE WASTE CRISIS
The Solutions

Scrap metal can be pressed into blocks and used for certain types of construction.

WHENEVER POSSIBLE, people should avoid creating wastes. Such source reduction of solid wastes conserves natural resources, saves valuable landfill and limits the need for incineration. Similarly, improving the quality of water before it is discarded makes both environmental and economic sense. Reducing the production of wastewater reduces the demands on treatment facilities, for wastewater must be treated if it is not to harm the environment. The degree of treatment that is desirable depends on the contaminants in the water. Silt and other suspended solids are relatively easy to remove by chemical means. Biological processes decompose organic matter, and the addition of chlorine destroys disease-causing bacteria. Most difficult—and costly—is removing toxic chemicals.

Right: Wastewater is aerated by giant turbines at a U.S. treatment facility.

FACTORIES AND OTHER INDUSTRIAL OPERATIONS often have their own wastewater treatment plants. In some cases, these are the same as municipal plants. In other cases, they use special processes to reduce the concentration of dangerous chemicals. By changing their manufacturing processes, in-

dustries may be able to limit the production of toxic wastes. For example, the chlorine in bleach used to whiten paper reacts with wood during the pulping process to produce deadly dioxin. New technologies decrease the use of chlorine, which in turn reduces the amount of dioxin in wastewaters.

Below: Treated wastewater is used for processing pulp at a paper mill.

SOURCE REDUCTION—NOT PRODUCING WASTES IN THE FIRST PLACE—is the best way to eliminate the amount of wastes. The next best alternative is recycling. This is the process of using something over and over again or of converting discarded materials into new products. Recycling conserves energy and natural resources, preserves our waste-disposal capacity, cuts pollution and saves money. Newspapers, cardboard, glass and plastic bottles, metal cans, garden debris,

Left: Boxes of paper products sit by the curb, awaiting pick-up by a neighborhood recycling program. *Above*: Aluminum cans are compressed and tied into large cubes before they are recycled.

Above: Plastic diapers account for 2% of all U.S. solid waste. If a majority of parents used cloth diapers as an alternative, long-term solid waste could be significantly re-duced.

EACH YEAR, WE THROW AWAY BILLIONS of disposable diapers, plastic spoons and forks, batteries, ballpoint pens, razors and other products. While some people enjoy short-term benefits from the throwaway mentality, everyone shares in the long-term costs. Everyone can contribute to efforts that reduce wastes. Indeed, everyone has a responsibility to ensure that the world of tomorrow is not buried in the wastes of the present and past.

plastic fibers used in carpeting and as stuffing for vests, pillows, mattresses, furniture and sleeping bags. Recycled PET is also used to make molding, boat hulls, electrical wall sockets, nonfood containers and chemicals.

High-density polyethylene (HDPE), used for milk and juice jugs and for laundry detergent bottles, is recycled and used in the manufacture of nonfood bottles, flower pots, pails, crates, toys, pipe and sheet plastic.

Polystyrene foam is initially used for coffee cups, fast-food packaging and egg cartons. It can be recycled into garbage cans, memo holders, fence posts and "plastic lumber." In 1990, the state of Michigan and Dart Container Corporation announced that they would work together to recycle polystyrene coffee cups. More than 2.1 million polystyrene cups are purchased by the state annually for use by the employees and visitors to 80 state office buildings in the Lansing area.

As worries about saving our environment have intensified in recent years, communities around the world have stepped up implementation of large-scale recycling programs.

Recycling Metals

A brief look at three metals—iron, silver and aluminum—gives us an overview of what can be accomplished with recycling.

Iron and Steel

The recycling of iron and steel (a mixture of iron and other metals) has greatly increased over the past few decades. In large part this is due to the development of the electric arc steel furnace. This furnace uses electric energy to produce temperatures that reach 6,000°F (3,300°C). In a few hours, the scrap is melted and can be remolded into new steel. In the United States, the amount of steel produced by electric arc furnaces increased from 8% in 1960 to about 36% in 1990—all of it from recycled scrap.

Most of the iron and steel recycled in the United States and Canada comes from junked cars and appliances. A largely untapped source is steel cans—generally called tin cans because they have a thin tin coating. These cans are used as food and juice containers. They can be easily separated from other municipal wastes by using large magnets since iron is attracted to magnets but other materials are not.

Silver

The major user of silver is the photographic industry. A silver compound, silver halide, is the light-sensitive material in photographic film. After the film is exposed and processed, the silver ends up either on the exposed film or in the processing chemicals.

Among the largest consumers of film are the printing industry and hospitals and medical clinics that use X-ray film. Because silver is classified by the U.S. Environmental Protection Agency as a toxic pollutant, these users wish to limit the amount of it in their wastes. Also, they wish to recycle silver because of its monetary value. One system that can be used is Du Pont's Silver Management Program. Under this program, Du Pont picks up exposed film from its customers, takes it to one of its plants and separates the silver from the film base. The film base can be recycled, too. Du Pont also collects the spent processing chemicals, using a cartridge system that extracts the silver from the other chemicals.

One user of Du Pont's program is Baystate Medical Center in Springfield, Massachusetts. This hospital conducts about 200,000 X-ray procedures each year. According to Walter Kroll, the hospital's radiology service engineer, before beginning to use the Silver Management Program in 1988, the effluent had a silver content of 600 parts per million (ppm). With the program, said Kroll, "that soon dropped to below 2 ppm, and the last reading [in 1990] was 1.65 ppm."

Aluminum

In 1989, Americans used 81 billion all-aluminum beverage cans. They recycled 49.4 billion, or 60.8%, of these cans. This equalled 1,688 million pounds (766 million kilograms) of aluminum. According to the Aluminum Association, recycling these cans saved more than 12 billion kilowatt hours of electricity—the energy equivalent of some 20 million barrels of oil.

In addition to aluminum cans, other products are sources of recyclable aluminum. Among these are such consumer items as frozen food trays, pie plates, automobile parts, window frames, storm doors, siding and gutters.

Composting

Composting is a controlled process of decomposing organic matter, such as food scraps, grass clippings and plant material, into a dark brown, nearly odorless substance called humus. Humus is rich in nutrients needed by growing plants. It can be used instead of chemical fertilizers on lawns, farms and gardens. As a substitute for topsoil it has been used to restore lands after construction and strip mining. In sanitary landfills, it is used to cover layers of compacted garbage and to cap the landfills when they are closed. Compost is also used in parks, rangelands, golf courses, sod farms, commercial forests and along highways.

Common microorganisms, mostly bacteria and fungi, decompose the organic matter. They require moisture and plenty of air. As they feed on the organic matter, heat is generated and the compost becomes hot. This helps to kill a large number of disease-causing bacteria that may be present in the material. Once the decomposers deplete the food supply, heat generation slows and the pile cools.

Composting begins by forming a pile of the wastes. One commonly used method is the windrow. A windrow is an elongated pile several feet high. The wastes are periodically turned to expose more of the material to air. Another method is a rectangular pen made of woven wire such as chicken wire. Again, the wastes must be periodically turned. Some people compost in large steel drums, punctured with holes and partially filled with wastes. To turn the material for aeration, the drum is simply rolled.

Most people think of composting as a pile of leaves and grass clippings in the backyard. Certainly, that is a convenient and easy way for people to recycle their own lawn debris. But there are other larger types of composting facilities: ones that can handle up to 800 tons of garbage a day.

By 1990, Florida had four large composting plants. The newest, in Pompano Beach, was the largest in the nation for turning municipal solid wastes into compost. It handled 400 tons of waste daily but expected to double this before the end of the year. The plant accepted almost all trash, including glass, metals, plastics, tires and diapers. Large items, such as rugs, tires and appliances, were removed and taken to a county landfill. Glass, metals and plastics were separated and pulverized into a sandlike material. The remaining wastes were shredded and composted in windrows. In several weeks, the wastes were decomposed and ready to be used throughout the state.

Any type of organic material can be composted. Some organic wastes decompose too slowly to be included in average compost piles, however. Experimenting often results in alternatives. William Brinton, president of Woods End Research Laboratories in Mount Vernon, Maine, figured out how to compost the shells of crabs caught off the coast of Florida. He found that the addition of wood wastes would speed decomposition of the crab wastes—thereby helping to turn

BUILD YOUR OWN COMPOST PILE

It's easy to make compost at home. Below is one procedure for making a compost pile. There are many variations on this, however. Once you have made several compost piles, you will probably develop your own "recipe."

1. Clear a level area in a corner of your yard. The area should be about 3 feet (0.9 meter) square.

2. Make a bin out of chicken wire and scrap wood. Leave one side of the bin open for easy access.

3. Place coarse brush at the bottom of the pile. This—plus the chicken wire—lets air circulate through the material.

4. On top of the brush, place a layer of plant material, including grass clipping and leaves.

The layer should be 6 to 10 inches (15 to 25 centimeters) deep. Many kitchen scraps, including egg shells and coffee grounds, can be added to the compost pile. Used mulch, wood ashes, sawdust and sod can also be added. Don't add meat, bones or fatty foods—they attract animals. Small scraps decay more quickly, so you may wish to consider shredding leaves and other wastes.

5. If the compost pile is near a home, you may wish to add a few inches of alfalfa meal or cat litter to help absorb odors.

6. Cover with a layer of soil, dried leaves or manure 2 to 3 inches (5 to 7.5 centimeters) deep.

7. Repeat this layering sequence

until the pile is several feet high.

8. Composting requires air and moisture. Turn the material with a pitchfork every few weeks to distribute air and moisture. If the center of the pile becomes dry, add water to it as you turn it over. The pile will feel hot and worms may be seen; these indicate that the natural decomposing process is working.

9. The compost is done when it becomes a dark crumbly material that is uniform in texture. In most climates, this takes 3 to 6 months. But it may take only several weeks—or an entire year. When it is ready, spread the compost on the lawn, around trees and under shrubbery. Work it into flower beds before planting. And use it as potting soil.

Florida's annual yield of 3,000 tons of crab scrap into salable fertilizer.

Another problem is the presence of toxic materials in compost. Pesticide residues do not appear to be a problem; apparently they break down during composting. Heavy metals are another matter. If lead, mercury and other heavy metals are in the end product, its use is limited. It may be acceptable for spreading on landfills but landscapers and farmers will not use it. Increasingly, state and other regulators are requiring that the finished product of compost plants be tested for purity.

Encouraging Recycling

Manufacturers will use recycled materials and make recyclable products if there is a stable supply of the materials and a stable market for them. Everyone, from an individual consumer to a giant corporation or government agency, can encourage recycling—by returning items for recycling and by buying items made from recycled materials.

WHAT CAN BE RECYCLED?

Construction Waste, Tires
Reprocessed for Pressed Board, Roads and other Construction Projects

Plastics, Drink Bottles
Reprocessed for Auto Parts, Fiberfill, Strapping

Glass
Refilled or Cullet for Jars, Bottles, Construction Material

Aluminum Cans
Reprocessed for Can Sheet and Castings

Furnishings and Clothing
Reused by Another Person

Animal Waste
Used as Fertilizer

Other Metals
Cleaned and Reprocessed as Scrap and Structural Products

Yard Waste
Composted for Landscaping

Paper (Mixed Paper, High-Grade Paper, Newspaper, Cardboard)
Reprocessed as Newsprint, Paperboard, Insulation

Organizations that buy large quantities can be especially effective in building markets for recycled goods. Most environmental organizations are committed to using recycled and recyclable materials. Government and private organizations are removing "virgin only" clauses from their buying policies. The EPA prints most of its publications on recycled paper, buys hand towels and toilet paper made from recycled material, and in 1990 began using copier paper made of at least 50% recycled fibers.

Frequently, large organizations have switched to recycled materials as a result of pressure from individuals. Students have convinced school boards, diners have convinced restaurants, shoppers have convinced supermarkets, employees have convinced employers, and so on.

Governments encourage recycling with tax credits and loans for industries that use or process recycled materials. For example, Florida implemented a 10 cent-per-ton waste recovery fee on virgin newsprint—and a 10 cent-per-ton tax credit for use of recycled newsprint.

Governments can encourage consumers to return recyclable materials by requiring deposits. For example, some states have bottle bills, which require consumers to pay a refundable deposit on glass and aluminum beverage containers.

Sometimes, mandatory recycling systems are established. In Rhode Island, every employer of more than 500 people must submit to the state its plan for reducing and recycling its wastes. In California, newspapers published in the state will be required to use recycled newsprint for at least 25% of their needs by 1993 and 50% by 2000. At least 10 states and more than 500 cities in the United States now have mandatory recycling programs.

Education is also important. Many people do not understand how they contribute to the waste crisis—and how they can help solve this crisis. They do not understand how wastes hurt their health and cost them money.

Some people want to recycle, but they find it difficult to determine what is recyclable. For example, most people cannot distinguish between different types of plastics. One solution, adopted by many states, is to have manufacturers stamp standardized codes onto plastic containers to help consumers identify the type of plastic used.

Reduce, reuse, recycle: these are the three R's that must begin waste management programs. It can be done. Indeed, it is being done by individuals, businesses, communities and nations around the world. Everyone has a responsibility to contribute to these efforts and to encourage their growth. Everyone has a responsibility to ensure that the world of tomorrow is not buried in the wastes of the present and past. As we accept responsibility to reduce wastes, conserve resources and protect the environment, the waste crisis will diminish. We will have created a brighter, healthier future for ourselves and for the planet on which we live.

GLOSSARY

activated carbon A highly absorbent form of carbon used to remove odors and toxic substances from gaseous emissions. In advanced waste treatment systems, it is used to remove dissolved organic matter from wastewater.

aerobic A biochemical process that depends on the presence of oxygen.

anaerobic A biochemical process that occurs in the absence of oxygen.

asbestos A mineral fiber that can cause cancer if inhaled or ingested.

background radiation Radiation from natural radioactive materials, such as uranium and radon in soil; it is always present in the environment.

biochemical oxygen demand (BOD) The amount of dissolved oxygen needed by microorganisms to decompose organic matter in water. It is a measure of pollution because heavy waste loads have a high demand for oxygen.

biodegradable The ability of a substance to decompose through the action of microorganisms into simple, stable compounds such as carbon dioxide and water.

bloom A population explosion of algae in a body of water, often as the result of pollution such as runoff from farmlands and landfills.

carcinogen A substance that causes cancer.

chlorinated hydrocarbons A class of persistent, broad-spectrum insecticides, including DDT, aldrin, heptachlor, mirex and others.

chlorination The application of chlorine to drinking water, sewage and industrial wastes to disinfect the material or to oxidize undesirable compounds.

coliform bacteria Bacteria found in the intestinal tract of humans and animals. Their presence in water is an indication of pollution.

compaction Reducing the volume of solid wastes by rolling and tamping.

compost Decayed organic matter that can be used as a fertilizer or soil conditioner.

corrosion A reaction between a chemical and a metal that breaks down the metal.

decomposition The breakdown of matter into simpler substances by bacteria and other means.

detergents Synthetic washing agents. Most detergents contain large amounts of phosphorus, which upon entering lakes and rivers may kill useful bacteria and encourage algal growth.

dioxins A group of extremely toxic chemicals. Some are formed as by-products during the manufacture of pesticides and other substances. They may also form during the incineration of wastes.

dump A site used for the disposal of solid wastes without environmental controls.

effluent Water discharged into the environment from an industrial plant or wastewater treatment facility.

eutrophication The aging process of a lake, during which it evolves into a marsh and eventually disappears; human activities that add nutrients to a lake can speed up the process.

fallout Radioactive material that falls out of the atmosphere in dust or precipitation.

feedlot A relatively small, confined area for raising cattle that results in lower costs but may concentrate large amounts of animal wastes that cannot be absorbed by the soil, thus resulting in runoff that pollutes nearby waterways.

fertilizer A nutrient added to the soil to improve plant growth.

fossil fuels Coal, oil and natural gas formed from the remains of organisms that lived millions of years ago.

genetic engineering The process of inserting new genetic information into existing cells to modify the characteristics of an organism.

groundwater Water under the surface of the earth. It fills aquifers and supplies wells and springs.

half-life The time needed for half the quantity of a substance to disintegrate. For example, the half-life of radium is 1,580 years; the half-life of DDT is 15 years.

hazardous wastes Wastes that may cause illness or death or pose other hazards to human health or to the environment.

heavy metals Metallic elements such as mercury, lead, arsenic and cadmium. Even at low concentrations they can harm organisms.

high-level wastes Waste materials that are highly radioactive, such as spent fuel from a nuclear reactor.

holding pond A pond or reservoir used to store polluted water.

humus Decomposed organic material.

incineration The disposal of wastes by burning.

isotopes Different forms of the same chemical element; they have different numbers of neutrons (but the same number of protons) in the nuclei of their atoms.

leachate Material that pollutes water as it seeps through solid wastes, as in mine tailings or a landfill.

low-level wastes Waste materials that emit low levels of radioactivity.

mutagen A substance that causes genetic changes.

NIMBY Acronym for "Not In My Back Yard." It describes people's opposition to the siting of such facilities as landfills and other waste disposal operations in their community.

oxidation The combining of oxygen with other elements. Combustion and respiration are processes that involve oxidation.

PCBs (polychlorinated biphenyls) A group of toxic chemicals used in transformers and capacitors.

pesticide A substance used to control undesirable insects and other pests.

pH A measure of the acidity of a substance; it is represented on a scale of 0 to 14, with 7 being a neutral state, 0 most acid, and 14 most alkaline.

phenols A class of compounds that contains carbon and hydrogen.

phosphate A chemical compound containing a group of one phosphorus and four oxygen atoms, as in sodium phosphate (Na_3PO_4).

pollutant Anything introduced into the environment that harms the environment or the usefulness of its components.

polychlorinated biphenyls (PCBs) *See* PCBs.

precipitators Air pollution control devices that collect particles from an emission by mechanical or electrical means.

radioactive wastes Wastes that spontaneously emit particles or rays.

radioisotope A radioactive form, or isotope, of an element.

radon A naturally occurring radioactive element formed by the decay of radium.

recycling The process of using something over and over again or of converting discarded materials into new products.

rem (roentgen equivalent man) The unit used to measure the amount of exposure from a dose of radiation.

repository A permanent disposal facility for high-level nuclear wastes.

reprocessing The process by which spent nuclear fuel is separated into waste material for disposal and reusable material such as uranium and plutonium.

sanitary landfill A waste-disposal method. Garbage and other solid wastes are spread in thin layers, compacted by heavy machinery and covered with soil daily.

scrubber An air pollution control device that uses a spray of water to trap pollutants and cool emission.

septic system An underground sewage system. It consists of a tank and a soil absorption field. It depends on bacterial decomposition and other natural processes to dispose of the wastes.

sewage Organic wastes and wastewater produced by residential and commercial establishments.

sewer A channel or pipe that carries wastewater and storm-water runoff from the source to a treatment plant or receiving stream.

shielding Materials—such as concrete, water and lead—that are placed around radioactive materials to protect people against the danger of radiation.

sludge A semi-liquid residue that remains after sewage is treated.

soil conditioner Humus, compost or another organic material added to soil to increase water absorption, build a bacterial community and distribute nutrients.

spent fuel Fuel that has been used in a nuclear power plant's reactor to the point where it no longer contributes efficiently to the nuclear chain reaction; it is still highly radioactive and can be reprocessed.

strip mining A recovery process in which coal or other mineral deposits are removed from the earth's surface by shallow excavation, in contrast to deep tunnel mining; large quantities of waste tailings are produced during the process.

tailings Waste materials created during mining operations.

teratogen A substance that causes birth defects.

thermal pollution The discharge of heated water from industrial plants, which threatens the life processes of aquatic organisms.

toxicity The degree of danger posed by a poisonous substance to human, animal or plant life.

toxic waste Waste materials containing poisonous chemicals.

uranium A radioactive element that is the basic fuel of a nuclear reactor.

urban runoff Storm water from city streets, usually carrying litter and organic wastes.

wastewater Water carrying dissolved or suspended solids from homes, farms, businesses and industries.

water pollution The presence of materials in water that damage its quality.

water supply system The collection, treatment, storage and distribution of drinkable water from source to consumer.

FURTHER READING

Blumberg, Louis, and Robert Gottlieb. *War on Waste: Can America Win Its Battle with Garbage?* Washington, DC: Island Press, 1989.

Brown, Michael H. *The Toxic Cloud*. New York: Harper & Row, 1987.

Cohen, Gary, and John O'Connor (eds.). *Fighting Toxics: A Manual for Protecting Your Family, Community, and Workplace*. Washington, DC: Island Press, 1990.

Crampton, Norm. *Complete Trash*. New York: M. Evans and Co., 1989.

Earthworks Group. *50 Simple Things You Can Do to Save the Earth*. Berkeley: Earthworks Press, 1989.

Elkington, John, Julia Hailes, and Joel Mackower. *The Green Consumer*. New York: Penguin Books, 1990.

Epstein, Samuel S. *Hazardous Waste in America*. New York: Random House, 1983.

Gibbs, Lois Marie. *Love Canal: My Story*. Albany: State University of New York Press, 1982.

Goldstein, Eric A., and Mark A. Izeman. *The New York Environment Book*. Washington, DC: Island Press, 1990.

Harris, Christopher, William L. Want, and Morris A. Ward. *Hazardous Waste: Confronting the Challenge*. Westport, CT: Greenwood Press/Environmental Law Institute, 1987.

Hynes, H. Patricia. *EarthRight*. Rocklin, CA: Prima Publishing & Communications, 1990.

Lave, Lester B., and Arthur C. Upton. *Toxics, Chemicals, Health, and the Environment*. Baltimore: Johns Hopkins University Press, 1987.

League of Women Voters. *The Nuclear Waste Primer*. New York: Nick Lyons Books, 1985.

Moore, Andrew Owens. *Making Polluters Pay: A Citizens' Guide to Legal Action and Organizing*. Washington, DC: Environmental Action, 1987.

Null, Gary. *Clearer, Cleaner, Safer, Greener: A Blueprint for Detoxifying Your Environment*. New York: Villard, 1990.

Rifkin, Jeremy (ed.). *The Green Lifestyle Handbook*. New York: Henry Holt & Co., 1990.

Robinson, William P. (ed.). *The Solid Waste Handbook*. New York: John Wiley & Sons, 1986.

Sardinsky, Robert. *Resource-Efficient Housing Guide*. Snowmass, CO: Rocky Mountain Institute, 1989.

Vyner, Henry M., M.D. *Invisible Trauma: The Psychosocial Effects of Invisible Environmental Contaminants*. Lexington, MA: D. C. Heath & Co., 1988.

Periodicals that regularly cover issues associated with waste management:

BioCycle: Journal of Waste Recycling. P.O. Box 351, Emmaus, PA 18049.
Environment. Heldreff Publications, 4000 Albemarle Street NW, Washington, DC 20016.
Garbage: The Practical Journal for the Environment. 435 9th Street, Brooklyn, NY 11215.
Greenpeace. Greenpeace USA, 1436 U Street NW, Washington, DC 20009.
Science News. Science Service, 1719 N Street NW, Washington, DC 20036.
Sierra. Sierra Club, 730 Polk Street, San Francisco, CA 94109.

INDEX

Chlorofluorocarbons (CFCs), 19
Cholera, 7, 72
Cities, 28
Closed-loop process, 94
Colorado, 8, 45, 58
Columbus, OH, 26
Compaction, 22
Composting, 99-101
Connecticut, 17
Consumers, 85-87
Corrugated cardboard, 95
Cottingham, Robert, 35
Cravath, Swaine & Moore, 92
Cyanide, 78

D

DDT, 31-32, 38, 70
Decommissioning, 63
Deep well injection, 44-45
Denmark, 52, 89
Denver, CO, 8, 45
Deposit bottles, 11, 81, 103
Detroit, MI, 27
Diapers, 81
Digestive disorders, 52
Dioxins, 16, 25, 34, 38-40, 46, 83, 89
Direct Marketing Association, 85
Diseases. *See* Health problems; specific diseases
Disposable products, 16, 17, 86
Down's syndrome, 54
Dysentery, 7

E

Earthquakes, 45, 62
Eastern Europe, 19
Effluent, 16, 77
Electricity, 26
Emissions, 25, 26-27
England. *See* Great Britain
Environmental Protection Agency (EPA), 8, 28, 33, 47
Erie, PA, 45
Europe, 14, 26
  see also Eastern Europe; specific countries
Eutrophication, 70-72

F

Factories, 19, 78
Farming, 16, 66
Fertilizers, 16
Finland, 51
Fish, 8, 54, 67, 69-70, 78
Flammable chemicals, 34
Floc, 76
Florida, 94, 100, 103
Fly ash, 25, 26, 47
Food
  contamination of, 34, 40, 54
  packaging of, 17-18, 40, 86, 89, 98
  processing of, 16, 44, 78, 85
Food chains, 34, 54, 69-70
Fossil fuels, 19
France, 24, 51, 59, 63
Fresh Kills, NY, 7, 27
Fuel rods, 57, 59
Fungi, 99

G

Gamma radiation, 52, 53
Garbino, Jenny Pronczuk de, 34
Gardner, Martin J., 55-56
Gas, heating, 27
Gastroenteritis, 72
Gene disorders, 54
Genetic engineering, 85
Germany, 24, 51, 59, 69, 72, 89, 96
Glass recycling, 94
Gochfeld, Michael, 24
Governments, 89, 103
Grand Junction, CO, 58
Great Britain, 51, 56, 92
Greenhouse effect, 19
Greenpeace, 10, 95
Groundwater, 44, 76

H

Hagarsville, Ontario, 93
Half-life, 53
Hanford nuclear plant, 51, 54, 58, 59, 63
Hazardous wastes
  alternatives to, 87
  disposal of, 43-49

monitoring of, 47
  types of, 31-41
  see also Radioactive wastes
Health problems, 7-8, 35-37, 39-40, 46, 48, 54-56, 72-73
  see also specific problems e.g., Cancer
Heavy metals, 25, 35-36, 69, 77, 78, 101
Hepatitis A, 7, 72
High blood pressure, 36, 73
High-density polyethylene (HDPE), 17, 84, 97
High-grade paper, 95
High-level wastes, 57
Household wastes, 23, 40-41, 87
Humus, 99
Hydrocarbons, 38

I

Incineration, 10, 25-27, 29, 46-47, 78
India, 95
Industrial wastes, 6, 15-16, 19, 35, 43, 66, 82-85
Infectious wastes, 14, 29, 47
Inland Sea, 72
Integrated waste management, 28
Iron, 98
Isotopes, 53
Italy, 72, 89

J

Japan, 51, 55, 59, 70, 72, 92, 93
Junk mail, 85

K

Keep America Beautiful, 13
Khian Sea (ship), 10
Kidney disorders, 41
Kroll, Walter, 99

L

Landfills, 6, 10, 22-24, 27, 44, 60-61
Lasers, 18
Latin America, 72
Leachate, 22-23
Lead, 15, 33, 35, 73, 101

Photo Credits

Page 4, © Gene Daniels/National Archives; p.12, © Robert A. Isaacs/Photo Researchers, Inc.; p.20, © David M. Dennis/Tom Stack & Associates; p.30, © David M. Doody/Tom Stack Associates; p.39, © Steven L. Waterman/ Photo Researchers, Inc.; p.42, AP/Wide World Photos; p.50, © Grant Heilman; p.64, © Barbara Burnes/Photo Researchers, Inc.; p.67, Metcalf & Eddy Companies, Inc.; p.71, Philadelphia Museum of Art, Smith Kline Beechman Corp. Fund © 1981, The Heirs of W. Eugene Smith, courtesy of Aileen M. Smith; p.74, © Grant Heilman; p.80, © Paul O. Boisvert/Seventh Generation; p.90, © Steve Elmore/Tom Stack & Associates; p.93, Oxford Energy

Cover, portfolio opener/Problems, © Larry Lefever/Grant Heilman; portfolio page 2-3, © Louis Goldman/Photo Researchers, Inc.; portfolio page 4, Envirosource; portfolio page 5, © T. Kitchin/Tom Stack & Associates; portfolio page 6, © L. Nicholson/Photo Researchers, Inc.; portfolio page 7, © Holt Confer/Grant Heilman; portfolio page 8, © Jack Swenson/Tom Stack & Associates.
Portfolio Solutions: Opener, Proler International Corp.; portfolio pages 2-3, © Brian Parker/Tom Stack & Associates; portfolio pages 4-5, © Gary Milburn/Tom Stack & Associates; portfolio page 6, © Steve Elmore/Tom Stack & Associates; portfolio page 7, Alcoa; portfolio page 8, National Association of Diapering Services.

Photo Research by Photosearch, Inc.